MW00396897

## Forward

I didn't set out to write a cook book because I'm a better cook than anyone else. I wanted to leave our Assyrian children a historical reference whose origins began in ancient Assyria. Other people tried to come to Assyria to compete for land, power and influence, but none would completely succeed in conquering Assyria and Assyrians. We maintained our ethnic identity through all the conquests, (the Greeks, the Romans, the Persians, the Ottomans, the UK, the Arabs, the Kurds, USA, even Genghis Khan, and Saddam), not to mention Christianity itself. We kept writing, educating, perfecting, documenting and passing it on to generations of Assyrians to come. We maintained our way of life, living in the garden of eden, whom the universe had blessed with every grain, plant, and tree, domesticating all sorts of life for our consumption and building life on earth. However, the entire world would benefit from our civilization. It spread "to the four corners of the world" as Kings of Assyria would say and write for us on clay tablets. And why not? The bible tells us so. Assyria became bigger and eventually the most powerful nation on earth in her time. All other civilizations inherited the Assyrian one. The traditions of the world can be traced all the way back to Assyria, BAB El, the Gate of God, Babylon, in the Assyrian Empire, out of which human civilization and language was born and spread around the globe.

Authentic Assyrian Recipes Cook Book is unique in its approach to reproducing the original flavors our Assyrian ancestors created. This book focuses on herbs and spices used to recreate those original flavors. The recipes used in this book were compiled from my family's traditional dishes made by my paternal grandmother Anna Yonan who was born in Geog Tapa, Urmia, fled the Assyrian genocide and married in Baghdad, Iraq, and lived there most of her life until she moved to Chicago in 1959, my maternal grandmother Sanam Putros, who was born in Satlowe, Urmia but also fled the genocide and married in Baghdad but went back to Satlowe for most of her adult life, until her return to Basra as a middle-aged mother, and of course my amazing mother, Jean Kardalia Yonan, who was born in Baghdad but lived in Satlowe with her mom until their return to Basra, and ended up marrying my dad, Rabee Youab I Yonan in Baghdad in 1946. They had 4 children in Iraq, two girls, then two boys, and in 1966 moved their family to Chicago. Everything I learned about Assyrian cuisine came from my mother who preserved these recipes that she learned from her own mother and mother-in-law.

In honoring their memory, by sharing their recipes, their cooking style and healthy cuisine presentations for all families to enjoy, I hope to create a book that emphasizes a healthy kitchen as the foundation of a healthy life. My goal is to preserve the ancient recipes developed by my ancestors and give the gift of health and empowerment to all people to use to serve nutritious and delicious meals to their families. The flavors of these dishes tell an old story, developed in various regions of Assyria by a people who strived to perfect all of their inventions and discoveries.

In ancient Assyria, spices were used in daily life, even present on the table in little bowls to be sprinkled on various foods, just as the herbs were used to eat raw green foods to compliment their cooked food and to add extra layers of flavor, making sophisticated dishes to please even the royal palate. One of the most common usage of spices as condiments was cumin.

Cumin's popularity in ancient Assyria is also evident in the world's oldest recipe collection, the Yale Culinary Tablets, which date to about 1750 BC. Written in Assyria, what is now Iraq, the tablets attest to the Mesopotamians' taste for highly spiced food with lots of onions, garlic and kamûnu, as cumin was called in Akkadian, the Semitic language the recipes were written in and from which the Assyrian language comes.

Almost a millennium later in the 9th century BC, the Assyrian king Ashurnasirpal II threw a huge feast to celebrate the construction of his new capital, Nimrud, in what is now northern Iraq. Boasting about it in a royal inscription erected in his new palace, Ashurnasirpal lists the massive quantities of food he served to guests from all over his empire, including lots of cumin. It was probably used as a table condiment even back then, just as it still is throughout the Middle East.

Many nationalities have claimed some of the Assyrian dishes in this book, but the names and origins of herbs and spices used in these ancient Assyrian recipes, as well as the names of these foods tell the real story. None of the modern languages existed when Assyrians were domesticating these plants. Neither did these modern states exist back then such as Iraq, Iran, Turkey, Jordan, Syria, etc. All these nations adopted our recipes and modified them according to what was available to them. We did not take from them, they took from us. Overtime, they made our recipes their own. Here's a quote from James Wiener, "One should mention too that ancient Mesopotamian cuisine shaped the cuisine of the ancient Persians, medieval Arabs, and Ottoman Turks."

The French Assyriologist and gourmet chef Jean Bottero, wrote "The three Akkadian tablets, dating to about 1700 BC, revealed, a cuisine of striking richness, refinement, sophistication and artistry, which is surprising from such an early period. Previously we would not have dared to think a cuisine 4,000 years old was so advanced. Various cooking techniques were known, and a complex assortment of herbs and spices was used to flavor a single dish. Garnishes and presentation were so highly esteemed that they were mentioned in recipes that are otherwise not highly detailed. In one recipe, crumbled bread provided a thickening. And, just as modern cooks collect recipes from other regions or countries, the Mesopotamian chefs gave credit to the Assyrians."

Towards the end of this book, I have included some of the recipes written by our Assyrian ancestors on clay tablets. It is remarkable that not much has changed in the way Assyrians cook even today, and the ingredients and techniques used are nearly identical.

It looks like I have come full circle as an Assyrian, documenting and preserving our heritage for future generations, just the way my Assyrian ancestors did before me. If I stumble a little, forgive me. I am writing this book as I watch my mother's health fail. I'm about to lose the most precious word in the world, "Mother." I will never have my mother for the rest of my life. As an Assyrian, I can say I have done my best to do my part, to keep this Assyrian tradition going and honor my mother and all of my ancestors.

As a human being I can say the Assyrians had the greatest civilization, the greatest food, the greatest culture, which is why everyone wanted to conquer it but in the end was transformed by it. Remember when Alexander the Great came to Babylon, he was shocked to find a highly advanced culture that was living in splendor while his people lived in squalor, despite his teacher's warning, that he was going to the land of barbarians. Alexander was so enthralled with our culture, its opulence and majesty that he never left. He died in Babylon, eating, drinking and living in Assyria.

It is my hope that Saroyan is right, that "everyone in the world is an Assyrian, the son of that great race" the race of man.

Ann-Margret "Maggie" Yonan
September 24, 2019

Dedicated to my beloved parents Jean and Youab Yonan who gave me the gift of life in Assyria and taught me the true meaning of love, and to my precious son Shmoel, who stole my heart the minute I met him in my arms, and had the honor and privilege to be his mother.

Graduation day at California State University, Northridge-1986. Three of the most precious people in my life.

# Table of Contents

## ASSYRIAN SPICES

Most Assyrian recipes use fresh or dried herbs and spices. The main spices used in Assyrian cuisine are the following:

-Beebar Koomta (Black pepper).
-Karry (Curry powder)
-Baharat (aka All spice, or 7 Spices or gram masala)
-Biryani spice
-Coriander Seeds-Bazra d'Toleh khsheeleh
-Zarda "Curcum" (Turmeric)
-Hail (Cardamom)
-Beebar smooqta (red pepper/paprika/cayenne)
-Za'afaran (Saffron)
-Shibit (Dill seed)
-kamûnu (Cumin)
-Smooqa/Sumac ܣܘܡܩܐ (red sour tannen powder). See picture next page
-Jinjafel (Cinnamon)
-Meekhaka (Cloves)

Some of the ancient recipes written on clay tablets by the Assyrians hint at how curry powder was used, just by reading some of the ingredients listed in their recipes.

**Making your own Curry Powder**

1 tsp Coriander seed roasted and cooled
1/4 tsp Cardamom seed
1/2 tsp ground cumin roasted and cooled
1/2 tsp ground ginger
1/2 tsp ground mustard seeds
1/4 tsp ground cloves
1/4 tsp ground Fenugreek
1/2 tsp Turmeric
1/4 tsp chilli powder
1/2 tsp Peppercorn
2 Star Anise
Combine all ingredients and grind into a powder. This mixture can be stored in a tight jar and will last a month. After that, the taste and the aroma subside.

**Making your own Bahart**

5 tablespoons mild paprika
4 tablespoons ground black pepper
3 tablespoons ground cumin
2 tablespoons ground coriander (Cilantro seeds)
2 tablespoons ground cinnamon
2 tablespoons ground cloves
1 tablespoon ground cardamom
1 tablespoon ground star anise
1 teaspoon ground nutmeg

It is best to grind your own, and if not possible, then buy them already ground and mix all the above, and store in a jar with a tight lid and refrigerate. This will last you for several weeks. After that, the smell and the flavor will begin to subside.

Sumac is another delicious flavor Assyrians use for its tanginess, especially with meat, such as kabobs. I used to get it from the homeland and grind my own, but this is readily available in Middle Eastern stores already processed.

## ASSYRIAN HERBS

From the Akkadian herbal texts we understand that herbs were not only used widely in cooking, but served on ancient Assyrian tables and functioned as appetizers and digestives. Assyrians still use a lot of herbs in cooking and they also compliment cooked food with fresh herbs served on the table not only to add layers of flavor to the cooked food but the vitamins we get from eating fresh herbs. Do not underestimate the nutritional value of fresh herbs. In fact, parsley has 33 times the amount of vitamin C, 16 times the amount of vitamin K, six times the amount of iron and four times the amount of calcium as lettuce. Other fresh herbs, such as basil, chives, mint, tarragon, cilantro and dill have high amounts of vitamins, antioxidants and minerals, too. The most used herbs for Assyrian cooking are the following:

-Shibbit (Dill)-
-Madanos (flat leaf Parsley)
-Toleh (Cilantro)
-Iryane (Basil)
-Ninkha (Mint)
-Mazra (Savory)
-Talkhoun (Tarragon)
-Bisleh qeeneh (green onions)
-Kawar (chives)
-Purpookheena (Purslane)
-Tooma (Garlic)
-Bisleh (Onions)
-Sutreh (Thyme)

Basil-(Iryaneh)-There are two kinds of Basil; the green sweet kind in this picture, and the purple kind. It doesn't matter which one you use in Assyrian cooking. The purple basil is stronger, more aromatic.

Cilantro-(Toleh)-Is a strong and fragrant herb Assyrians use in a variety of foods, either fresh or dried. We also use crushed Cilantro seeds (coriander seeds) in our cooking.

Dill-(Shibit)-Belongs to the Anise family. We use it fresh when available or freeze it for when it is not available. We also use dill seeds for pickling and the star anise to make spices with.

Flat leaf Parsley-(Madanos)-Fresh or dried, this is widely used in Assyrian cooking-It is full of chlorophyl and therefore nutritious as well as a good antiseptic and cleanser.

Mint-(Ninkha)- Comes in 17 different varieties. The most commonly used in Assyrian cooking is Spearmint.

Here's a quote from scholars translating Assyrian tablets, "Mint was used by the ancient Assyrians in rituals to their fire god."

Purslane-(Purpookheena)-Is odorless herb but has a distinct tanginess and can be combined in a variety of salads or can be cooked. It grows wild and most people think it is a weed, but it is edible and quite meaty. It adopts any flavor you give it and has a tangy bite and soft texture, easy to digest. It grows rampant in California.

Savory-(Mazra)-A very subtle aroma and therefore blends well in cooking and gives a delicious fragrance and flavor. It can be used fresh or frozen and mostly used by Assyrians for dolma and Kipteh.

Terragon-(Talkhoon)- Has a subtle smell but adds a strong and delicious flavor to cooked food. It can be used in poultry or meat dishes but Assyrians mostly use it in dolma and Kipteh.

Kawar-Chives or baby leeks-These are from my garden-Used to add onion/garlic flavor, raw or cooked, therefore very sought after for those who are garlic intolerant.

Bisleh Qeeneh-Green Onions-These are from my garden-Unbeatable in adding an extra layer of flavor to any meal, and the aroma it gives in cooked food.

Shitla d'Shanbata-Fenugreek was domesticated in Assyria also. Charred fenugreek seeds have been recovered from Tell Halal, today's Iraq, carbon dated to 4000 BC as well as the Bronze Age settlements of Assyria in Lachish. We use the fresh or dried leaves to cook in stews and we crush and grind the seeds for other uses. It is a very strong and aromatic herb.

Fenugreek

In our family, we serve gillaleh (herbs) with all rice and stew dinners. Gillaleh are part of each dinner table and mostly consist of Tolleh (Cilanto), Iryaneh (Basil), bisleh qeeneh (green onions), Madanos (parsley), beebar qinta (sweet or hot green pepper), poulleh (radishes). We clean them, de-stem the herbs, wash them in a bowl a few times and strain them each time. After straining them in a colander, I usually lay them flat on a clean kitchen towel, then wrap them up in that towel and put them in a sealed plastic bag to refrigerate until I'm ready to serve them on the table. These herbs are very fragile and they wilt in heat. Gillaleh or herbs are healthy, nutritious, and antiseptic, besides being delicious and aromatic.

Each of these herbs contribute a certain flavor and aroma to the dish which without would not taste authentic or even good. It is why it's extremely important that we preserve these ancient recipes and not only pass them down to future Assyrian generations but make them available to the world so they can eat delicious, nutritious, healthy meals using basic and accessible ingredients the ancients used to build a spectacular and lasting civilization. As the famous American author and playwright William Saroyan wrote, "In a sense, everyone in the world is an Assyrian, a son of that ancient race" for the simple fact that civilization came out of Babel, BAB EL (the Gate of God).

The ancient Assyrians preserved ancient Assyrian recipes on clay tablets thousands of years ago and we must do the same. We must be the link to that continuity. We can't get these flavors from any other nationality. They didn't use herbs and spices the way the Assyrians did. Cooking is an art and art needs practice and practice makes perfect, and the Assyrians perfected these recipes over thousands of years. I hope you'll enjoy cooking these ancient recipes in your own kitchen, for your own families and developing a taste and a love for healthy eating and living.

Herbs that can be frozen after de-stemming, washing, straining and drying in a towel then store them in a sealed plastic bag before freezing:
Talkhoun-Tarragon
Mazra-Savory
Kawar-chives must be chopped before freezing
Shibbit-Dill

Herbs that need to be dried because they're too fragile for freezing:
Toleh-Cilantro
Madanos-Flat leaf parsley
Ninkha-mint
Iryani-basil

Assyrians also use seeds either whole or grind/crush into flavors used for cooking and baking. Some of them are:

Toleh seeds crushed (Cilantro Coriander dry seeds)
Mayana whole (Nigella seeds)

Yarqa dry seeds whole (Caraway seeds or dry dill seeds)
Shishma (Sesame seeds)

**Other flavors used in Assyrian cooking are:**
Rose Water
Orange blossom water
Tamarind
Pomegranate juice or syrup
Sour cherry juice or syrup
Date syrup
grape syrup
Grape molasses
Date molasses
Orange zest
Lemon zest

**Tamar Hindi**-(Date of India) Tamarind is rich in minerals (Potassium, Phosphorus, Magnesium and Calcium) as well as vitamins Niacin and Thiamin. Assyrians of today's Iraq use it a lot in cooking. Originally I did not know its benefits but I've loved the flavor and richness it adds to dishes, which is why I have used it a lot in my cooking, as did my Assyrian ancestors.

Don't buy tamarind paste. It's old and as it ages it gets too dark to use in cooking. Buy it fresh, peel it, soak it in water for a few hours or even overnight and use it fresh or store in a jar in the refrigerator for a few weeks. Then when you need more, make a new batch. This will not only give you the original flavor and color intended for some of our Assyrian dishes, but you'll get the nutrients as an added benefit.

In a small bowl combine 6 peeled tamarind pods and 1 cup water. Soak 2-3 hours. Mash to remove the seeds and stems. Mix the sauce until the water and tamarind combine. Strain through a mesh sieve and store in a sealed jar in the refrigerator. This will last you a few weeks.

## ASSYRIAN STEWS-Shirwa

In ancient Assyria, traditional Assyrian stews were made with lamb. But many people (like me) don't like the lamb smell and taste, which is why I use beef in all my dishes. These recipes can be substituted with lamb for those who like the flavor. The ingredients listed can be easily found in all stores around the world. Stews are nutritious and good source of fiber. Since stews are cooked vegetables, Assyrians compliment them with raw herbs for their nutritional value as well as their cleansing properties, not to mention they add extraordinary layers of flavors to cooked food.

No other nationality has this much variety of stews like the Assyrians. The Persians only have a few stews that are well known, such as Qorma Sabsi and Qeemeh and Green bean stew is mostly made by Assyrians of Iran. India has a variety of stews but not many compared to the Assyrians. In fact, the Assyrians are given credit for most Middle Eastern stews and influenced all modern Middle Eastern cooking, including the Persians, the Arabs, and the Turks.

Some Assyrians don't eat every stew with rice. They eat them with bread as in the old days. Additionally, many Assyrians substitute rice with burghul, (cracked wheat), which is more nutritious and has more fiber and very little starch.

This book includes recipes made with bulghur.

**Shirwa D'Lobia (Green bean stew)**

Lobia stew is made by both Iraqi and Persian Assyrians, This recipe is Iraqi Assyrian.

1 pound beef stew cut up 1 inch each
1 pound green beans washed, stems removed and cut up bite size.
2 large minced onions
1 sweet green pepper (your preference) chopped.
4 stalks of celery washed and chopped
2 tomatoes washed and chopped
1/2 cup madanos (flat leaf parsley) washed and chopped
1 teaspoon curry powder
1 tablespoon paprika
1/2 teaspoon black pepper
2 cloves crushed garlic
1/4 teaspoon turmeric.
1/4 cup oil
14 cups water, 10 for the meat, 4 for the stew
2 teaspoons salt
1 8-oz can of tomato paste

STEP 1-In a large pot, heat 2 tablespoons of oil. Add meat and 1 minced onion and sauté until meat browns. Add turmeric and sauté 2 minutes. Add 10 cups of water to the sautéed meat and 1 teaspoon salt. Stir and bring to boil. When the pot boils, skim the foam that rises to the top, then lower the flame, cover the pot and let it simmer until most liquid is evaporated and meat is tender (about an hour). Do not let the meat burn.

STEP 2-When the water is all evaporated, to the meat pot add the rest of the oil and heat on high. Add 1 minced onion, the crushed garlic, and 1 chopped green pepper and sauté together in the same pot, (3-4 minutes). Add 1 teaspoon curry powder, 1 tablespoon paprika, 1 teaspoon salt, 1/2 teaspoon black pepper and stir 2-3 minutes. Add the diced tomatoes and stir continuously 2-3 minutes. Add 1 small can of tomato paste and sauté 2-3 minutes. Don't let the mixture dry out.

STEP 3-Add the green beans, the chopped celery, and sauté 2-3 minutes. Add 4 cups of water and stir. Cover the pot and bring to boil for 6 minutes. Reduce the heat and let simmer on low for 20-30 minutes, stirring occasionally. When the sauce thickens and the green beans are cooked, remove from heat and allow to rest for 10 minutes before serving. Serve over white rice and enjoy with gillaleh-

NOTE-Salt and black pepper to taste. You can reduce or increase the salt, depending on your dietary restrictions. I don't like too much salt and if you're a heavy salt user, it tends to make this dish slightly bitter when it's too salty. Start with smaller amounts and work your way up until it tastes good for you, You can keep tasting as you cook until you feel it's the right amount of salt, but wait till the end, to add more salt than the recipe calls for.

## Yakhnee (Garbanzo Bean stew)

This is strictly an Iraqi Assyrian dish

1 pound of beef stew cut up
3 medium potatoes, peeled, washed and cut up bite size
2 cans of garbanzo beans, drained of liquid
2 minced Onions
1 Green pepper of any kind, chopped
4 large chopped tomatoes
1 teaspoon paprika
2 teaspoons turmeric
1/2 teaspoon black pepper
1 teaspoon salt
14 cups of water
1 8-0z can tomato paste
1/4 cup oil

Step 1-In a large pot over high flame, add 2 tablespoons of oil, the meat and 1 minced onion and sauté until meat is brown. Add 1 teaspoon turmeric and sauté 1 minute. Add 1 teaspoon salt and 10 cups of water to the sautéed meat. Stir well and bring to boil. Skim any foam that rises to the top and discard. Boil for 10 minutes. Reduce heat, cover the pot and simmer the meat on low (1 hour).

Step 2-When all the water is evaporated, add the rest of oil, 1 minced onion, the crushed garlic, and 1 chopped green pepper and sauté together in the same meat pot, (3-4 minutes). Add the paprika and sauté another minute. Add the turmeric and sauté 1 minute. Add the tomato paste and stir for 2-3 minutes. Add the garbanzo beans and the cut up potatoes and sauté for 3 minutes. Add 4 cups of water, salt, pepper and stir well. Cover the pot and bring to boil for 6 minutes. Reduce heat and simmer on low for 30 minutes. Once the sauce is thickened and the potatoes are cooked, remove from heat and let stand for 10 minutes before serving.

Serve with your favorite bread and enjoy with gillaleh, or tourshi.

## Shirwa d'Bomia (Okra Stew)

This is strictly an Iraqi Assyrian dish

1 pound beef stew cut up
1 pound small size okra, fresh or frozen depending on season
2 large minced onions
1 green pepper chopped
5 cloves crushed garlic
1/4 cup oil
2 teaspoons of salt
1 tablespoon paprika
1 teaspoon turmeric
1/2 teaspoon black pepper
1 8-oz can tomato paste
14 cups of water.
the juice of 1 lemon

Step 1-In a large pot over high flame, heat 2 tablespoons oil on high. Add the meat and 1 minced onion and sauté until meat is brown. Add 1 teaspoon turmeric and sauté 1 minute. Add 1 teaspoon salt and 10 cups of water to the sautéed meat and bring to boil for a few minutes so that you can skim the foam that rises to the top. Reduce heat, cover the pot and simmer the meat on low (1 hour).

Step 2-When all water in the pot is evaporated and the meat is tender, add the rest of oil, 1 chopped onion, 1 chopped green pepper, all the crushed garlic and sauté 2-3 minutes. Add paprika, salt and black pepper and sauté for another minute. Add one can of tomato paste and stir well, letting it cook 2-3 minutes. Add 4 cups of water, the okra and lemon juice. Stir well and bring to boil for 6 minutes. Reduce heat and simmer for 30 minutes on low. When okra is tender, and the sauce has thickened, remove from heat and let the pot rest for 10 minutes before serving.

Serve over white rice and enjoy with gillaleh.

**Sheikh M'Hashy** (Stuffed Eggplant stew). This is strictly an Iraqi Assyrian dish meaning 'Stuffed Sheikh' in Arabic, but the origin of this dish is Assyrian. Eggplant was one of the items offered to guests of the most famous feast held by the Assyrian King Ashurnasirpal II in the ninth century BC and Iraqis know this history.

6 Japanese eggplants cut in half width wise, making two eggplants
1 pound lean ground beef (93% lean or better)
2 large minced onions
10 cloves crushed garlic
1 bunch madanos (flat leaf parsley) washed and chopped
2 tablespoons Baharat (All spice or Gram Masala)
1/2 cup oil for frying
2 teaspoons salt
1/2 teaspoon black pepper
1 8-oz can tomato paste
3 cups water

The Stuffing
Step 1-In a large frying pan with a cover, heat 2 tablespoons oil to coat the pan. Add the ground beef and slightly brown, breaking it down. Add 1 minced onion, 1 bunch chopped parsley, 6 cloves of crushed garlic, 1 teaspoon salt, 1/2 teaspoon black pepper, 1 tablespoon baharat and stir well until all ingredients are cooked. Transfer the meat to a bowl and set aside to cool.

Step 2-Wash, de-stem and cut the eggplants in half width wise. With a coring tool remove the insides of the eggplants. Save the insides for the sauce. Sprinkle salt on each cored eggplant and set aside for 15 minutes. This kills the bitterness.

Step 3-To a clean saucepan, add the rest of oil and heat well. Add the hollowed out eggplants and fry slightly on all sides (1 minute on each side). Remove from the frying pan and set aside on a plate. Allow all vegetables to cool.

Step 4-Chop the insides of the eggplant and fry in the same oil 3-5 minutes. Add 4 cloves of crushed garlic, and 1 minced onion. Sauté well 3-5 minutes. Season with 1/2 teaspoon salt, 1/2 teaspoon black pepper, and 2 tablespoons baharat. Sauté for 6-8 minutes or until the chopped eggplants are broken down to a smooth consistency. Add one can of tomato paste and sauté 3 minutes. Add 3 cups of water and stir well, cover and bring to boil for 2 minutes. Reduce heat and let simmer while you stuff the eggplants.

Step 5-Stuff all vegetables tightly with the sautéed meat and lay all of them one by one in the simmering sauce. If there's some meat left over, throw it into the sauce. Spoon some of the sauce from the bottom of the pan onto the stuffed eggplants, covering them with sauce. Cover the pan and simmer on low for 30 minutes. When my guests are late, I keep the Sheikh M'hashy in a warm oven. Serve over white rice and enjoy with gillaleh.

**Assyrian Kipteh (Meatball Stew)**

Kipteh is an Assyrian national dish.

Optional- hard boiled eggs (1 for each meatball)
Also optional is 1 chopped zucchini in the sauce

The Meatballs

1 pound extra lean ground beef
1/2 cup of fine Burghal #1 soaked in water for 1/2 hour.
1 large minced onion
1 tablespoon dried Iryani (basil) OR 1/2 cup fresh basil chopped
1 tablespoon dried Mazra (Savory) or 2 tablespoons fresh or frozen savory chopped
1 teaspoon Talkhoun (Tarragon)
1 teaspoon salt
1 tablespoon paprika
1/2 teaspoon black pepper
.

In a large bowl combine 1 pound lean ground beef, 1 minced onion, 1 tablespoon fresh or dried Iryani (basil), 1 tablespoon fresh or dried mazra (Savory), 1 teaspoon sTerragon, 1 teaspoon salt, 1/2 teaspoon black pepper. Mix well. Squeeze out all the excess water from the fine #1 burghal and combine with the meat. Mix well. (Some Assyrians like to form large meatballs out of this mixture by putting a hard boiled egg in each meatball. I do not like eggs so I don't use them.) Form medium sized meatballs and set aside.

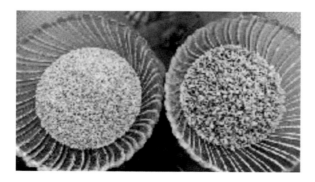

Picture-On the left is fine burghal # 1. On the right is coarse burghal # 4. Before soaking

The Sauce
1/3 cup #4 coarse Burghal soaked in warm water for 1/2 hr
1 large minced onion
2 tablespoons Iryani (purple basil), washed and chopped or 1 tablespoon dried basil
1 tablespoon mazra (Savory)
1 teaspoon talkhoun (Tarragon)
1 jalapeno (whole) or any sweet green pepper you have on hand
1 8-oz can tomato paste
7 cups of water
1 tablespoon salt
1 tablespoon paprika
1/2 teaspoon black pepper
1/4 cup oil

In a large pot, add 1/4 cup oil and heat. Add 1 minced onion and sauté for 3-5 minutes. Add paprika and stir well. Add one can of tomato paste and stir well. Cook for 2 minutes. OPTIONAL-Add 1 chopped zucchini and sauté for 1 minute. Add 7 cups of water. Squeeze all the water out of the soaking coarse burghal #4 and add to sauce. Add the salt, pepper, Iryani, Talkhoun and mazra and bring sauce to a rolling boil.

Begin to drop the meatballs into the sauce very gently. Once all the meatballs are in the pot, add the whole jalapeño or any whole green sweet or hot peppers you like to the sauce. Let the pot boil 10 minutes. Then cover the pot and let it simmer about 30 minutes.

Sauce should neither be too thick or too thin. If too thick, add boiling water to it. The consistency should be similar to a thick soup.

My paternal grandmother, Anna Yonan liked to make the Kipteh using whole hot pepper in the sauce. She thought hot peppers are an antiseptic to any germ, especially when you have a cold. She also used hard boiled and peeled eggs inside each meatball.

Serve the dish in bowls. Enjoy with Lawasha, (Assyrian cracker bread) and gillaleh

**Kubba Hamouth** (Stuffed Dumpling Stew)

This is strictly an Iraqi Assyrian dish developed in Nineveh, (what is today northern Iraq). The original word used in Assyrian clay tablets is Kubbusu.

The Dumpling Dough

1 1/2 cups rice flour
1/2 cup Cream of wheat
1 pound extra lean ground beef
1 teaspoon Salt
1/2 teaspoon black pepper
4 cloves crushed garlic
1/2 cup water

Combine dry ingredients and mix well. Add the ground beef and crushed garlic and mix well. Start adding a little bit of water at a time and work the dough with your hands until you achieve a pink doughy consistency. Don't make the dough too wet or too dry. Cover and refrigerate until ready to use.

The filling-
1 pound extra lean ground beef
1 large minced onion
8 large cloves of crushed garlic
1 bunch parsley, de-stemmed, washed, strained and chopped
1 tablespoon curry powder
1 teaspoon salt
1/2 teaspoon black pepper

Brown the ground beef, breaking it down with a wooden spoon. Add minced onions, crushed garlic, chopped parsley and cook for 3-4 minutes. Add salt and pepper and curry powder. Cook for another 2 minutes. Set aside to cool.

The sauce-
1/4 cup oil
1 large minced onion
1 large zucchini cut bite size
4 tablespoons dried mint
2 tablespoons Tamarind sauce
1 8-ounce can of tomato paste
1 8-oz can of tomato sauce
1 tablespoon curry powder
1 tablespoon paprika
1 tablespoon salt
1/2 teaspoon black pepper

10 cups of water.

In a big pot, heat 1/4 cup oil. Add one large minced onion, and sauté for 2-3 minutes. Add the paprika and sauté for another minute. Add the curry powder and sauté for 1 minute. Add the tomato paste and tomato sauce and sauté for 2-3 minutes. Add the chopped zucchini and sauté for another 2-3 minutes. Add 10 cups of water, salt, pepper, the tamarind, the dried mint and stir well. Bring to a rolling boil. Turn heat down and let it simmer on low while you make the kubbas.

Take a pinch of dough and form into the size of a golf ball. Stick your thumb into the ball of dough and enlarge the hole by rotating the ball in your other hand so you can add filling into the hole. Spoon 1-2 tablespoons of filling and put it inside the dough. Close the dough together like a dumpling using water to wet your hands and make the kubba round shape and flat like a disk, or like a torpedo or like a ball. Make sure there are no open holes. If you see the dumpling opening, add a tiny bit of dough on the hole and use water to repair the tear. Once all the kubba/dumplings are made, bring the sauce to a rolling boil. Add the kubba to the sauce, one a time. When the kubba rises to the top it is cooked. Let it simmer for a while until the sauce slightly thickens. Let the stew rest for 10-15 minutes before serving.

Some people use sliced raw turnips instead of zucchini. It depends on your taste. I add zucchini because they pick up the kubba flavor, whereas turnips add a different layer of flavor to the kubba, so that's why I don't use turnips. But it's up to you.

This is my mother's recipe. If you like it spicy add 1/2 teaspoon cayenne to the sauce or one jalapeño to the sauce before it starts to boil.

This recipe serves at least ten people, sometimes more. If you want to cook half of the Kubbas only, you can freeze the rest to cook in sauce for another time. They freeze well, but the sauce doesn't. Enjoy with gillale and any kind of bread you like.

**Kubba Yakhni**-Kubba Hamouth in broth

Some Assyrians make kubba Hamouth in broth instead of tomato based sauce. Follow the same Kubba Hamouth recipe for making the dough and the stuffing.

The sauce
1 pound beef or lamb with bone
1 bunch spinach de-stemmed, washed and chopped
2 potatoes peeled and cut up
1/4 cup oil
1 minced onion
1 teaspoon baharat
1 can garbanzo beans strained
1 teaspoon dry mint
1 tablespoon salt
1/2 teaspoon black pepper
1/4 cup lemon juice

In a large pot filled 3/4 of the way with water, add 1 tablespoon salt, all the meat, 1/2 teaspoon pepper corn, and bring to boil. With a slotted spoon, remove all the foam that is rising to the top of the pot. Cover the pot and simmer for 1 hour until the meat is tender.

When the meat is finished cooking, in a saucepan heat 1/4 cup oil on high. Add the minced onion and the baharat and sauté 2-3 minutes until onions are soft. Add the cut up potatoes and the spinach and sauté 2-3 minutes. Add the sautéed mixture to the meat pot. Add the drained garbanzo beans, the lemon juice and the dry mint and bring to a rolling boil. When the broth comes to a boil, add the kubbas one a time. Stir very carefully so the kubbas don't come apart. When the kubbas rise to the top, they are cooked.

Serve with Samoon, tourshi and gillaleh

**Ras A'sfoor** (Curried Meatball Stew)-This is strictly an Iraqi Assyrian dish

The Meat Balls:
1 pound extra lean ground beef
1 large minced onion
5 cloves crushed garlic
1/3 cup plain bread crumbs
1/2 bunch madanos (flat leaf parsley) de-stemmed, washed, strained and chopped
1 teaspoon curry powder
1/2 teaspoon salt
1/4 teaspoon black pepper
1/2 teaspoon turmeric

In a bowl, combine all ingredients and mix well. On a cutting board sprinkle some flour. Make small meatballs out of the meat mixture (the size of a bird's head, which this dish is named for). Roll the meatballs in the flour to cover the meatballs well.

The Sauce:
1 large minced onion
1/3 cup oil
2 tablespoons curry powder
1 teaspoon salt
1 teaspoon turmeric
1 tablespoon paprika
1/2 teaspoon black pepper
4 medium potatoes, peeled, washed and cut bite size.
1 minced onion
1 green pepper chopped
3 cloves crushed garlic
4-5 cups water
1 8-oz can tomato paste

In a large pot, add 1/3 cup oil and heat on medium flame. Add the cut up potatoes and fry until golden. Remove the potatoes with a slotted spoon and set them aside. Fry the meatballs in the same oil, stirring gently to fry on all sides. Remove meatballs from oil and set them aside. To the remaining oil in the pot, add the minced onion, chopped green pepper, crushed garlic and sauté 2-3 minutes. Add 2 tablespoons curry powder, 1 teaspoon turmeric, 1 tablespoon paprika and sauté 2 minutes. Add the tomato paste and sauté for 2 minutes. Add the fried meatballs, the fried potatoes and stir to mix. Add 4-5 cups of water, 1/2 teaspoon black pepper, 1 teaspoon salt, and stir well. Bring to boil for 5 minutes, then turn heat low, cover the pot and let simmer for 20-30 minutes, checking occasionally to see if the sauce has thickened. Allow to rest 5 minutes before serving. OPTIONAL-Some Assyrians add 1 cup peas to this dish. Peas add a sweetness to this dish, that's why I don't use them.
Serve over white rice and enjoy with gillaleh and tourshi

**Karee d' kteta** (Chicken Curry Stew)

This is strictly an Assyrian Iraqi dish.

4 chicken breasts cut into bite size
4 medium size potatoes peeled, washed and cut up bite size
1 minced onion
5 cloves crushed garlic
1 large green pepper chopped
1 8-oz can tomato paste
2 tablespoons curry powder
1 teaspoon turmeric
1 teaspoon salt
1/2 teaspoon black pepper
4-5 cups water
1/3 cup oil

Step 1-In a large pot, heat up the oil and add the cut potatoes and fry till light golden brown. With a slotted spoon remove the potatoes from oil and set them aside.

Step 2- To the remaining oil add 1 minced onion, the crushed garlic, chopped green pepper and sauté 2-3 minutes. Add the cut up chicken and sauté until no longer pink. Add turmeric, curry powder, salt and black pepper and sauté for 2 more minutes. Add the tomato paste and sauté for 2-3 minutes. Add the fried potatoes, and 4-5 cups of water and stir the pot well. Bring to boil for 6 minutes. Reduce heat and let simmer 20 minutes until sauce thickens. Allow to rest 5 minutes before serving.

Serve over white rice and enjoy with gillaleh.

**Karry d' Bisra** (Beef Curry stew)

This is strictly an Assyrian Iraqi dish

1 pound beef stew cut up
4 medium potatoes cut into bite size
1 large minced onion
1 large green pepper chopped
5 cloves crushed garlic
1 8-oz tomato paste
2 tablespoon curry powder
2 teaspoons turmeric
1 teaspoon salt
1/2 teaspoon black pepper
1 tablespoon Paprika
14 cups of water
1/3 cup oil


In a large pot over high flame, heat 2 tablespoons oil. Add the meat and 1 minced onion and sauté until meat is brown. Add 1 teaspoon turmeric and sauté 1 minute. Add 1 teaspoon salt and 10 cups of water to the sautéed meat and bring to boil for 10 minutes, removing the foam that rises to the top. Reduce heat, cover the pot and simmer the meat on low (1 hour).

When all the water is evaporated, add the rest of the oil to the cooked meat, 1 minced onion, 1 chopped green pepper, 5 cloves crushed garlic and sauté for 2-3 minutes. Add paprika and curry powder and sauté for another minute. Add tomato paste and sauté 1-2 minutes. Add the cut up potatoes and sauté for 2-3 minutes. Add 4 cups of water, salt, black pepper and mix well. Bring to boil for 10 minutes, then reduce heat and let simmer for 30 minutes. Let rest for 10 minutes before serving

Serve over white rice and enjoy with gillaleh

**Tebsi** (meat and vegetable pie)

This is strictly an Iraqi Assyrian dish

The Meat:
1 pound ground beef
1 large minced onion
1 teaspoon turmeric
1 tablespoon paprika
5 cloves crushed garlic
1 teaspoon salt
1 teaspoon black pepper
1 teaspoon baharat

Mix all ingredients in a bowl, cover and refrigerate until ready to use.

The Vegetables:
4 large potatoes peeled, washed and sliced round like
4 Japanese eggplants washed and sliced round like
4 tomatoes washed and sliced round like
4 green peppers washed and sliced round like
5 onions peeled and sliced round like
1/2 cup oil

Spread all sliced vegetables on a cookie sheet and sprinkle with salt. When the vegetables sweat, pat dry with paper towel.

In a big frying pan heat 1/2 cup oil. Fry all sliced potatoes and set aside. Fry all sliced eggplants and set aside. Fry all sliced tomatoes and set aside. Fry all green peppers and set aside. Fry all sliced onions till golden and set aside.

The Sauce:
4 tablespoons oil
1 large minced onion
1 chopped green pepper
5 cloves crushed garlic
1 bunch parsley de-stemmed, washed, strained and chopped
1/2 teaspoon salt
1 tablespoon paprika
1/2 teaspoon black pepper
1 tablespoon baharat
1/2 teaspoon turmeric
3 cups water
4 tablespoons tomato paste

Preheat oven 350 degrees Fahrenheit

In a saucepan heat 4 tablespoons of oil. Add chopped onions, chopped green peppers, 5 crushed cloves of garlic and sauté 2-3 minutes. Add salt, pepper, paprika, baharat and turmeric and sauté. Add the tomato paste and sauté for 2-3 minutes. Add the chopped parsley and 3 cups of water and stir well. Bring to boil for 5 minutes and turn heat down and simmer on low.

Step 5-In a deep oven baking dish, sprinkle a bit of oil to coat the dish. Layer the meat flat into the pan and spread it evenly. Add a layer of sauce over the meat. Next, layer the fried potatoes. Add a layer of sauce over the layer of potatoes. Next layer the onions. Next layer the eggplants. Add a layer of sauce over the eggplants. Next layer the peppers over the eggplants. Next layer the tomatoes, and add sauce to cover all the vegetables.

Step 6-Place the pan uncovered into a preheated oven and cook for 30-40 minutes.

Serve over white rice and enjoy with gillaleh.

**Qaleta**-Fried vegetable Stew

4 eggplants sliced
4 Zucchinis sliced
4 tomatoes sliced
4 potatoes sliced
4 onions sliced
4 peppers sliced
1 minced onion
4 cloves crushed garlic
1 teaspoon turmeric
1 tablespoon paprika
1/2 teaspoon salt
1/2 cup oil
2 tablespoons tomato paste
1 cup water

Spread all the vegetables on a cookie sheet and sprinkle with salt.

In a frying pan add the oil and heat on high. Fry the potatoes on both sides till golden. Remove from oil and place in an oven safe dish. Fry the Eggplants and layer over the potatoes. Fry the zucchini and layer over the eggplants. Fry the onions and layer over the zucchini. Fry the peppers and layer over the onions. Fry the tomatoes and layer over the peppers. If you don't want to layer, you can mix all vegetables, as in the picture below.

In a saucepan heat 3 tablespoons oil and add 1 minced onion. Sauté until soft. Add the turmeric and paprika and sauté 1 minute. Add tomato paste, crushed garlic, 1 cup water, the salt and bring to boil. Reduce heat and simmer for 10 minutes. Pour the sauce all over the layered vegetables and bake in a preheated oven at 400 degrees Fahrenheit for 20 minutes. Serve over white rice.

**Shirwa d'Shabzi** (Herb stew with beef)

This is an Iraqi Assyrian recipe I'm using but the Persians make a similar dish called Qorma Sabzi, which is slightly different to the extent they don't use tomato paste or Cilantro in their stew and they use kidney beans instead of Black eyed peas.

1 bunch fresh flat leaf parsley, de-stemmed, washed, strained and chopped
1 bunch fresh Fenugreek cleaned, washed, strained and chopped
1 bunch fresh chives or young leeks de-stemmed, washed, strained, and chopped
1 bunch cilantro de-stemmed, washed, strained and chopped
2 large minced onions
2 cloves crushed garlic
4 tablespoons oil
2 teaspoons Turmeric
2 teaspoons salt
1 teaspoon pepper
1 cup oil for frying herbs
1 pound beef stew cut up
4 Noomie Basra (dried lime)
the juice of 1 lemon
1 heaping tablespoon tomato paste
1 can black eyed peas strained
13 cups of water
Virgin olive oil to your taste.

Step 1-In a big pot heat 4 tablespoons vegetable oil to coat the pot. Add 1 minced onion and sauté 2-3 minutes. Add the cut up beef stew and sauté till brown but juicy. Add 1 teaspoon turmeric and sauté 1 minute. Add 1 heaping tablespoon tomato paste and sauté 1-2 minutes. Add 1 teaspoon salt and 10 cups of water, and the dried lime. Mix well and bring to boil for 10 minutes. Reduce heat and simmer the meat on low for 1 hour. It should look like a meat gravy.

Step 2-In a big pot heat 1 cup oil. Add all the fresh chopped herbs and sauté 5-7 minutes making sure all herbs are coated and beginning to sweat some of the oil. Add 1 teaspoon turmeric and sauté another 2 minutes. Add the meat gravy to the sautéed herbs pot. Add 1 can of strained black eyed peas and stir well. Add 3 cups of water, salt, and lemon juice and stir well. Bring to boil for 10 minutes. Reduce heat and simmer on low for 1 hour. Let the pot rest for 10 minutes before serving. After the pot has rested for 10 minutes add 1/2 cup extra virgin olive oil and stir the pot well.

NOTE adding the virgin olive oil is optional. But I do add it every time, for several reasons: It is healthy, it makes the dish richer, more tasty, and adds some body to the cooked herbs.

Serve over white rice.

Herb stew (Shabzi) served with two kinds of rice and baked chicken

**Shirwa d'Mashe** (Red kidney Beans or white beans stew).

1 pound beef stew cut up
1 teaspoon salt
2 cans Red kidney beans or white beans, whichever you prefer
2 large minced onions
8 cloves crushed garlic
1 chopped green pepper
1 8-oz can tomato paste
1/4 cup oil
1 teaspoon salt
1 teaspoon turmeric
1 tablespoon paprika
1/2 teaspoon black pepper
15 cups water

Step 1-In a big pot, heat 2 tablespoons of oil. Add the meat, 1 minced onion and sauté 2-3 minutes. Add 1 teaspoon turmeric and sauté 1 minute. Add 10 cups of water and 1 tablespoon salt and bring to boil for 10 minutes. Reduce heat, cover and let simmer for 1 hour.

2-When the liquid is evaporated, add the rest of oil, 1 minced onion, the garlic, the chopped green pepper and sauté for 2-3 minutes. Add paprika and sauté for 1 minute. Add the tomato paste and sauté for 2-3 minutes. Add the kidney beans and 5 cups of water and bring to boil for 10 minutes. Add the salt and black pepper and stir well. Reduce heat and simmer for 30 minutes.

Iraqi Assyrians serve this dish without rice in a bowl. They poke a hole in the middle of the bowl and add 1 tablespoon Tourshi juice or apple cider vinegar and eat it with Samoon (Iraqi Assyrian bread looks like French rolls) but much lighter. They also serve this dish with Assyrian Tourshi (pickles). When they don't have Tourshi juice to add to the dish they add vinegar.

Some Iraqi Assyrians also serve this dish with a dollop of home-made masta tooma, garlic yogurt sauce.

You can also serve this dish over white rice and enjoy with gillaleh or Tourshi or both.


**Shirwa d'Qarreh** (Zucchini Stew)

1 Pound beef stew cut up
6 zucchinis washed and cut up bite size
2 large minced onions
3 cloves crushed garlic
1/2 bunch flat leaf parsley chopped
1 tablespoon curry powder
1/2 teaspoon cumin powder
1 teaspoon salt
2 teaspoons turmeric
1/2 teaspoon black pepper
1 tablespoon paprika
1 8-oz can tomato paste
13  cups water
1/4 cup oil
2 tablespoons Tamarind sauce OR the Juice of 1 lemon
1 tablespoon salt

Step 1-In a big pot, heat 2 tablespoons oil. Add the meat, 1 minced onion and sauté for 2-3 minutes. Add 1 teaspoon turmeric and sauté 1 minute. Add 10 cups of water and 1 tablespoon salt and bring to boil for 10 minutes. Reduce heat, cover and let simmer for 1 hour.

Step 2-Once the liquid is evaporated out of the pot, add 1/4 cup oil, 1 minced onion, crushed garlic, the chopped parsley and sauté for 2-3 minutes. Add 1 teaspoon turmeric, paprika, curry powder, and the cumin and sauté 2-3 minutes. Add the tomato paste and sauté 2-3 minutes. Add the zucchini and mix gently. Add 3 cups of water, 1 teaspoon salt, black pepper, 2 tablespoons tamarind sauce and stir. Bring to boil for 10 minutes. Cover and reduce heat to low and let simmer for 20 minutes. Serve over white rice and enjoy with gillaleh.

**Shirwa D'Qarnabeet** (Cauliflower stew)

1 pound beef stew cut up
1 cauliflower, washed, de-stemmed, and cut into florets (bite size)
1/2 bunch Cilantro, de-stemmed, washed, strained and chopped
2 large minced onions
1 tablespoon salt
1 8-oz can tomato paste
1 tablespoon curry powder
2 teaspoons turmeric
1/2 teaspoon baharat
1/2 teaspoon cumin powder
1/2 teaspoon ground coriander seeds
1/2 teaspoon black pepper
1 tablespoon tamarind sauce or the juice of 1 lemon
14 cups water
2 plums

Step 1-In a big pot, heat 2 tablespoons of oil. Add the meat, 1 minced onion and sauté for 2-3 minutes. Add 1 teaspoon turmeric and sauté 1 minute. Add 10 cups of water and 1 tablespoon salt and bring to boil for 10 minutes. Reduce heat, cover and let simmer for 1 hour.

Step 2-Once the liquid is evaporated, add 1/4 cup oil, 1 minced onion, crushed garlic and sauté for 2-3 minutes. Add 1 teaspoon turmeric, the paprika, curry powder, the cumin and baharat and sauté 2-3 minutes. Add the tomato paste and sauté 2-3 minutes. Add the cauliflower florets and mix gently. Add 4 cups of water, 1 teaspoon salt, 1/2 teaspoon black pepper, 1 teaspoon tamarind sauce, the plums and the chopped cilantro and stir. Bring to boil for 10 minutes. Cover and reduce heat and let simmer for 30 minutes. Let stand for 5 minutes before serving.

Serve over white rice and enjoy with gillaleh.

**Shirwa d'Qeema** (Ground beef stew)

1 pound extra lean ground beef
1 minced onion
1 chopped green pepper
4 chopped tomatoes
1/2 bunch cilantro de-stemmed, washed, strained, and chopped
2 tablespoons tomato paste
1/2 teaspoon curry powder
1/2 teaspoon baharat
1 tablespoon paprika
3 cloves crushed garlic
1/2 teaspoon turmeric
1/2 teaspoon salt
1/2 teaspoon black pepper
1/4 cup oil
3/4 cup water

In a large pan heat oil on medium heat and add the ground beef, breaking it down with a spoon and brown. Add the minced onion, the garlic and the chopped green pepper and sauté 2-3 minutes. Add the curry powder, the baharat, turmeric, paprika, salt and pepper and sauté 1-2 minutes. Add the chopped tomatoes and sauté 2-3 minutes. Add the tomato paste and sauté 2 minutes. Add the chopped cilantro, 3/4 cup water, salt and black pepper and sauté for another 2-3 minutes. Cover and reduce heat and let simmer for 10 minutes.

Serve over white rice or eat with your favorite bread and gillaleh

I also make sandwiches with it. Open a Samoom or french roll and stuff with qeema. Fill with gillaleh and enjoy with tourshi.

**Shirwa D'Leppi** (yellow split pea stew)

1 pound beef stew cut up
2 cups yellow split peas soaked for 1 hour, washed and strained.
2 large minced onions
3 cloves crushed garlic
1 chopped green pepper
2 teaspoons turmeric
1 teaspoon curry power
1/2 teaspoon black pepper
1/4 teaspoon cumin powder
3 noomi Basra (dried lime)
1 8-oz can tomato sauce
1/3 cup oil
14 cups water
2 tablespoons salt


Step 1-In a big pot, heat 2 tablespoons of oil. Add the meat, 1 minced onion and sauté for 2-3 minutes. Add the turmeric and sauté 1 minute. Add 10 cups of water and 1 teaspoon salt and bring to boil for 10 minutes. Reduce heat, cover and let simmer for 1 hour.

Step 2-When the liquid is evaporated, add 1/4 cup oil, 1 minced onion, 1 chopped green pepper, garlic and sauté 2-3 minutes. Add turmeric, curry powder, cumin powder, 1 teaspoon salt and black pepper and sauté 2-3 minutes. Add the tomato sauce and sauté 2-3 minutes. Add the split peas and sauté 1 minute. Add 4 cups of water and noomi Basra (dried lime) and stir well. Bring to boil for 10 minutes. Cover and reduce heat to let simmer for 30-40 minutes or until split peas are tender. Let stand 10 minutes before serving.

Spoon over white rice and sprinkle with chopped cilantro.

**Assyrian Tlokhe-Red Lentil Stew**

1 cup red lentils
1/2 cup rikta (Assyrian noodles) or you can use vermicelli noodles
1 minced onion
3 cloves crushed garlic
1 sweet green pepper chopped
1 tablespoon curry powder
1/2 teaspoon turmeric
1 teaspoon salt
1/4 teaspoon black pepper
3 tablespoons oil
4 cups water

In a large pot add the oil and heat on high. Add minced onion, green pepper and sauté 4 minutes. Add the turmeric and curry powder and sauté 1 minute. Add the red lentils, the noodles and garlic and sauté 2 minutes. Add the water and salt and stir well. Bring to boil for 5 minutes. Reduce heat and simmer on low until the lentils are soft and the sauce is slightly thickened.

Serve with your favorite bread and gillaleh

**Chillifry**

1 pound chopped sirloin
1 minced onion
4 cloves crushed garlic
1 green pepper chopped
1 tablespoon paprika
1/2 teaspoon black pepper
1 teaspoon salt
1/4 cup oil
1 8-oz can tomato sauce

In a large pot, heat 2 tablespoons oil and add the chopped beef. Stir fry till brown. Add the rest of the oil, the minced onion, chopped pepper, crushed garlic and sauté 2-3 Minutes. Add paprika and sauté 1 minute. Add tomato sauce and sauté 2 minutes. Turn heat to low and simmer covered 20 minutes.

Enjoy over rice or eat with bread and gillaleh and tourshi.

## Shirwa d'Bazalya (Green Pea Stew)

1 pound beef stew cut up
1 bag frozen peas
2 large minced onions
4 cloves crushed garlic
1 tablespoon cumin powder
1 tablespoon coriander powder (cilantro seed powder)
1 tablespoon curry powder
1/2 tablespoon black pepper
1 tablespoon paprika
1 tablespoon baharat
2 tablespoons tamarind sauce or lemon juice
1 chopped tomato
1 8-oz can tomato paste
2 teaspoons salt
1 teaspoon turmeric
14 cups water
1/4 cup oil

Step 1-In a big pot, heat 2 tablespoons of oil. Add the meat, 1 minced onion and sauté for 2-3 minutes. Add 1 teaspoon turmeric and sauté 1 minute. Add 10 cups of water and 1 teaspoon salt and bring to boil for 10 minutes. Reduce heat, cover and let simmer for 1 hour.

Step 2-When all the liquid is evaporated out of the meat pot, add the rest of the oil, 1 minced onion, and sauté for 2-3 minutes. Add paprika, cumin powder, curry powder, baharat, coriander powder, black pepper and sauté for 2-3 minutes. Add the chopped tomato and sauté for another 2 minutes. Add the tomato paste and sauté 2-3 minutes. Add the peas, and sauté 2-3 minutes. Add 4 cups of water, 2 tablespoons tamarind sauce or the juice of 1 lemon and 1 teaspoon salt and stir well. Cover the pot and bring to boil for 10 minutes. Reduce heat and let simmer on low 30 minutes or until sauce thickens.

Serve over white rice and enjoy with gillaleh.

## Shirwa d'Baqleh (Fava Bean/Broad Bean stew)

Assyrians of Iraq use peeled green Fava beans to cook this dish. If you can't find it use broad beans or canned green Fava beans.

1 pound beef stew cut up
2 cans green Fava beans, strained
1 minced onion
2 cloves crushed garlic
1 tablespoon paprika
2 teaspoons salt
1/2 teaspoon black pepper
1 8-oz can tomato sauce
2 tablespoons tomato paste
The juice of 1 lemon
1 tablespoon dry mint
3 noomi Basra (dried lime)
1/3 cup oil
14 cups of water


Step 1-In a large pot, heat up 2 tablespoons oil to coat the pot. Add the beef stew and onions and sauté for 3-5 minutes or until meat is browned. Add 10 cups of water, 3 noomi Basra and 1 tablespoon salt and bring to boil. Reduce heat, cover the pot and let simmer on low for 1 hour.

Step 2-When all the water is evaporated and the meat is tender, add remaining oil to the meat pot, 1 minced onion, the crushed garlic and sauté for 2-3 minutes, Add the paprika, salt, black pepper, and sauté 2-3 minutes. Add the tomato paste, the tomato sauce and sauté for 2-3 minutes. Add the Fava beans and sauté 2 minutes. Add the mint, the tamarind sauce or lemon juice, and 4 cups water and stir well. Bring to boil for 10 minutes. Reduce heat and let simmer for 30 minutes. Let the pot rest 10 minutes before serving.

Serve over rice or eat with bread and gillaleh

**Assyrian Harissa**-Assyrians serve Harissa for holidays and special occasions. My father's favorite meal is Harissa and Samoon.

1 whole chicken
1 cup barley washed
2 large minced onions
1 cup Irish butter
1 tablespoon salt

Step 1-Wash and clean the chicken and discard the gizzards. Place whole chicken, 1 minced onion inside a large pot filled 3/4 of the way with water. Bring to boil on high heat for 40 minutes. Take the whole chicken out of the broth and place on a deep tray or pan. Set aside to cool 30 minutes.

Step 2-Add washed barley to the boiling chicken broth while the chicken is cooling. When chicken is cool to the touch, pull chicken apart and discard all skin and bones. Shred the chicken into small pieces and add back into the pot. Put a tin under the pot and bring it to boil again, 5 minutes. Turn flame down to low and simmer for at least 5-6 hours, stirring occasionally and beating with a wooden spoon to break down the barley and the chicken. Do not allow the barley to stick to bottom of pot to scorch, which is why it's important you stir the pot often, and use a tin under it. When the chicken and barley have blended nicely together like a pasty soup, it is nearly done.

Step 3-Melt 1 cup Irish butter in a sauce pan. Add 1 minced onion and sauté 2-3 minutes. Cover the sauce pan and turn heat to low and allow the onions to simmer until caramelized. Add this to the chicken and barley mixture and stir well to combine. Simmer for an additional 2 hours, stirring and beating the chicken and barley mixture with a wooden spoon until completely blended. Add salt to taste.

You also have the option to combine the shredded chicken and barley pot and place the pot in the oven overnight at 300 degrees Fahrenheit. The Harissa will be nicely blended by morning. Then add the caramelized onions in Irish butter. Stir well and simmer on low with a tin under the pot for an additional hour.

Serve the Harissa in individual bowls. Drizzle with butter and sprinkle with crushed or ground birzara d'toleh (crushed coriander seeds). Enjoy with lawasha or Samoon.

## Assyrian Pacha-(Stuffed Tripe)-Reesh Aqleh
Tripe is the stomach of a sheep

Cleansing the pacha:

1 cow or sheep head
2 cow's feet or sheep feet
14 cups water

In a large pot combine all ingredients and bring to boil for 35 minutes. Strain and discard all liquid and set aside.

The broth:

1 lamb shank cut up into 6 pieces
3 noomi Basra (dried lime)
2 lemons quartered
10 cloves crushed garlic
1 minced onion
2 cinnamon sticks
3 tablespoons baharat
1 teaspoon turmeric
6 cardamom pods
1 tablespoon salt
1/2 teaspoon pepper
4 tablespoons oil
14 cups water

In a large pot add oil and heat on high. Add the minced onion and garlic and sauté 2 minutes. Add the turmeric, cardamon, cinnamon, and noomi Basra and sauté 2-3 minutes. Add lamb shanks and brown on all sides. Add 14 cups water and the cut up lemons and bring to boil. Add the cow head and feet and 1 tablespoon salt and cover and simmer for 2 hours, constantly skimming the fat that rises to the top.

The Stuffing

1 pound chopped beef stew
2 cups long grain rice soaked for 20 minutes
3 tablespoons baharat
1 teaspoon salt
1 minced onion
5 cloves crushed garlic
1/4 teaspoon black pepper
4 tablespoons oil

In a saucepan, add oil and heat on high. Add onion and sauté 2-3 minutes. Add the chopped beef and sauté till brown. Add garlic, salt and pepper and sauté 1 minute. Remove from heat and add the rice and mix well. Cover and allow stuffing to cool.

Cleansing the tripe
1 pound tripe
5 lemons sliced
1/4 cup flour
1/4 cup sea salt
1/4 cup white vinegar

In a large bowl combine all ingredients and mix well. Set aside for 30 minutes to cure. After 30 minutes, wash the tripe in cold water to remove all the flour. Strain the tripe in a colander to dry.

Filling and stuffing the tripe:

Cut the tripe into 6x6 inch pieces. Sew each one like a pocket, leaving an opening to fill the tripe. Fill the tripe with stuffing 3/4 of the way. Repeat with each piece of tripe. Now sew the tripe closed. When all the tripe pieces have been filled and sewn closed, pierce the tripe with a few small holes. Add to the simmering broth. Bring to boil, then turn heat down and simmer for another hour. Add 5 cloves crushed garlic and stir well.

Serving the Pacha;

In a large eating bowl, break 2-4 pieces of Assyrian flat bread. Place some stuffed tripe, and some shank over the broken bread. Spoon some broth over the meat. Add raw crushed garlic and enjoy with gillaleh and tourshi.

**Kashka By: Youno Atto Tower**

This recipe was contributed by Shushan Tower and it's her mother's recipe


1/2 Kilo or 2 1/2 cups wheat
100 grams or 1 cup red kidney beans
2 large onions roughly chopped
1 1/2 tea spoon salt
3 table spoon olive oil
50 grams or 1/4 cup salted butter
2 liters or 8 1/2 cups water
750g or 1 1/2 pounds Leg of lamb chopped large cubes include bone.

Method
Soak wheat in water for approximately two hours and put aside.

Place meat and 2liters or 8 1/2 cups of water in saucepan and cook for
approximately half an hour on medium to high heat and cover with lid. Then add
soaked drained wheat to meat in the saucepan. Cover with lid reduce heat to
medium for approximately two hours or until the wheat is well cooked. Add extra
boiled water should the wheat not be cooked tender.

Place red beans in separate saucepan add enough water to cover beans and
cook on medium flame until beans are tender.

Combine cooked and drained red beans in the cooked wheat and meat
saucepan.

In a frying pan, heat the olive oil and butter on high. Add the chopped onion
and cook until slightly browned. Add salt to the cooked wheat, meat, and bean
mixture and stir. Add the caramelized onions on top.

## ASSYRIAN RICE, BIRYANI AND BULGAR

Assyrians have many different recipes for rice. Some are plain,
sauce, and others very aromatic and spicy and yet others very fai.

Rice is a staple dish for the Assyrian people. Most days a normal housek
serving rice and some kind of stew, if they're not making dolma and other dei.
my grandmother Anna Yonan served rice even with dolma. That's how she was n
Urmia.

Whether you like Basmati rice or Jasmine rice like me, these rice dishes are sure to
please everyone. My son Sam was born in America and loves American, Italian and
Chinese food. But he loves Assyrian rice with any kind of shirwa, especially shirwa
d'Lobia with rizza (rice). So do my nieces and nephews who were all born in America
and some even have American mothers but they still love rice.

Many people believe Biryani originated in India. But that's not true. According to most
historians Biryani originated in Basra, Assyria, and when the sailors and laborers from
Bombay came in their boats to Basra harbor, they took this dish with them all the way
back to India. That's why to this day, Indians love Assyrian Biryani more than their own,
which is quite bland when compared to Assyrian Biryani.

On Wednesdays and Fridays, the Christian Assyrians don't eat meat. For the 40 days of
Lent and the fifty days prior to Christmas they don't eat meat either. They feast on Riza
Smooqa and zaladda, (Red rice and chopped salad). I can live on this food for the rest
of my life and the same with many members of my family. It is an Assyrian tradition that
was carried into Spain by the Arabs, then to Mexico when the Spaniards conquered it.
This is why Spanish rice is so similar to our Assyrian rizza smooqa.

Rice Smooqa therefore became famous the same way Biryani did, through trade on the
Silk Road and through conquests and labor migrations.

**Rizza**-Every Day Rice (Plain Assyrian white rice cooked stove-top)

2 cups Jasmine rice washed
3 cups water
1 tablespoon salt
1/3 cup of oil

In a large pot, bring three cups of water, 1/3 cup oil and 1 tablespoon salt to boil. Add
washed and strained rice to the boiling water, cover the pot and cook until water is
mostly evaporated, stirring twice so that the rice doesn't stick to the bottom of the pot.
Reduce heat to low and let simmer covered for 20-30 minutes. I use a flat tin under the
pot so the rice does not burn or stick to the pot.

Serve with any Shirwa (stew) and enjoy with gillaleh

**izza with Rikta** (Rice with Vermicelli-or Rice Pilaf) stove-top

2 cups Basmati Rice washed and strained
1/2 cup Vermicelli
1/3 cup oil
1 tablespoon salt
4 cups water

In a large pot heat the oil on high. Add the vermicelli and sauté for 2-3 minutes until golden brown. Add washed and strained rice and sauté 3-4 minutes constantly stirring. Add 4 cups of water, 1 tablespoon salt and stir. Cover the pot and bring to boil 6 minutes. Reduce heat and let simmer on low for 30-40 minutes or until the rice is tender.

Serve with any shirwa and enjoy with gillaleh

## Assyrian baked rice

Preheat oven at 350 degrees Fahrenheit.

4 cups Basmati Rice
1/4 cup sea salt
2 sticks butter melted
1 piece of lawasha or two pita breads
water

Fill a large pot with water, and 1/4 cup sea salt. When the water starts to boil, add 4 cups of washed rice. Bring to boil again. When the rice turns white (8 minutes) and before it cooks completely, strain the rice in a colander. You can test the rice with your fingers. Take a grain out of the boiling water and test it. If it splits in half with your nail, it's not ready to drain. If it is firm but doesn't split it's ready. Don't let the rice overcook.

In a large oven safe pot, add a few tablespoons of the melted butter and spread well covering the entire bottom of the pot. Add one piece of lawasha bread to the pot and press down to absorb the butter. Start layering the rice by spoon full at a time. Pour some of the butter over it and mix well. Spoon more rice into the pot and pour some butter over it and mix well. Add the rest of the rice and pour the rest of the butter over it and mix well. This should be done in 3 or four batches. Cover the pot with parchment paper and put the pot cover on. Bake the rice in a preheated oven for 30-40 minutes.

Optional-In a glass, combine 1/3 cup boiling hot water and 1 teaspoon saffron. Stir well and let marinade 15 minutes. Open the rice cover and pour the saffron on the rice in one long strip.  Bake an additional 10 minutes to make sure it is cooked well and fluffy. It should smell like popcorn.

Some Assyrians add some baked rice to the saffron and let the rice grains absorb the saffron. When the rice is served in a platter, they spoon some of the saffron rice over their rice plate.

Serving the baked rice-Spoon the baked rice onto a platter. Start scraping the bottom and breaking the fried bread. Layer the fried bread either on top of the rice or on the edges of the rice platter.

Serve with the stew of your choice.

## Assyrian Biryani

4 chicken breasts cut up bite size
1 pound lean ground beef
2 cups Basmati rice
4 medium potatoes peeled, washed and cut up bite size and salted
4 large sliced onions and salted
1/2 cup plain yogurt
10 cloves crushed garlic
3 tablespoons biryani spice
1/2 teaspoon black pepper
1 1/2 teaspoons salt
1 1/2 cup oil
1 minced onion
1 teaspoon turmeric
1/4 teaspoon ground cardamom
1/4 teaspoon ground cloves
1 tablespoon tomato paste
4 cups water

Step 1-Cut up chicken breast in bite sizes and put in a bowl. Sprinkle with 1/2 teaspoon salt and half of the crushed garlic and mix well. Add 1 cup plain yogurt and mix well. Cover and refrigerate for 1 hour.

Step 2-In a bowl, mix 1 pound lean ground beef, 1 minced onion, 1 teaspoon salt, 1 tablespoon biryani spice,1/2 teaspoon black pepper, three cloves crushed garlic. Mix well and form tiny meatballs (the size of marbles).

Step 3-In a large pot add 4 cups of water, 1 tablespoon biryani spice, 1 teaspoon salt, 1 teaspoon turmeric, the cardamom and cloves. Bring to boil and add the rice. Cook on high heat 8-10 minutes, stirring occasionally so the rice doesn't stick to the bottom of pot. When most of the water is evaporated, reduce heat to low and let the rice simmer 30-40 minutes with a tin under the pot.

Step 4-In a large frying pan add 1/2 cup of oil and heat on high. To the hot oil add the cut up potatoes and fry till golden. Remove the potatoes from the oil and set them aside. To the hot oil add the meatballs and fry the meat balls, on all sides, 5 minutes total. Remove the meatballs and set aside. To the remaining oil, add the sliced onions and fry until golden. Reduce heat and let the onions caramelize. Remove onions and lay on top of the fried potatoes and meatballs. To the remaining oil add the marinated chicken, 1 tablespoon Biryani spice, 1 tablespoon black pepper, the rest of the crushed garlic and sauté till the chicken is no longer pink. Mix 1 tablespoon tomato paste in a cup of water and add to the chicken. Mix well and sauté 2-3 minutes. Add the fried potatoes, the fried meatballs, the fried onions to the chicken pan and stir well, combining all ingredients. Let simmer on low 5 minutes.

Step 5-When the rice is done, add the meat mixture in its entirety to the rice pot and mix well. Let simmer on low for 20 minutes. Serve in big platter and enjoy with tourshi

**Basra Biryani**

4 cups Basmati rice
3 pounds beef stew cut up bite size.
2 tablespoons tamarind sauce
1/2 cup oil
4 medium potatoes peeled, washed and cut up bite size
4 large sliced onions
10 cloves crushed garlic
1/2 cup biryani spice
1/2 teaspoon black pepper
1 tablespoon curry powder
2 tablespoons baharat
1 tablespoon salt
1 cup oil
1 minced onion
1 tablespoon turmeric
1 tablespoon tomato paste
6 cups water

Biryani marinade
Step 1- In a small glass bowl mix 1/2 teaspoon curry powder, 1/2 cup Biryani spice, 1/2 cup oil, 1 tablespoon Tamarind sauce. Mix well and set aside.

In a pot add 2 tablespoons oil and heat on high. Add cut up beef stew and sauté till brown. Add 2 cups water and bring to boil. Reduce heat as soon as it boils and let simmer on low for 45 minutes. Add 1 tablespoon salt and 1 tablespoon Biryani marinade and mix well and cook for another 2-3 minutes.

Step 2- In a large pot, heat up 3 tablespoons oil, 1 tablespoon salt, 2 tablespoons Biryani marinade, 2 tablespoons baharat and sauté 1 minute. Add 4 cups washed and strained rice and sauté 2-3 minutes. Add 6 cups of water and bring to boil, until most liquid is evaporated. Reduce heat and simmer for 20 minutes.

Step 3-In a frying pan, heat 3 tablespoons oil and add the peas and 1/2 teaspoon salt and sauté 5 minutes. Add 1 tablespoon Biryani marinade and sauté another 2 minutes. Remove peas and set aside. To the hot pan add 2 tablespoons of oil and all the sliced onions and sauté till golden. Reduce heat and let the onions caramelize. Add 1 tablespoon Biryani marinade and sauté 2 minutes. Remove onions and set aside.

Preheat oven at 350 degrees Farenheit

Step 4-In a roasting pan with cover, place parchment paper on the bottom of the pan. Layer half the cooked rice, pressing it down with a wooden spoon. Layer all the meat on top of the rice, pressing it with a wooden spoon. Layer all the onions on top of the meat, pressing it with a wooden spoon. Layer all the peas on top of the onions, pressing it with a wooden spoon. Add remaining rice and press it all down with a wooden spoon. We're trying to achieve a mold by pressing every layer down. Add another piece of parchment paper and cover the pot. Bake in the oven for 30 minutes. Remove the pan from the oven and let it rest for 5 minutes. Remove the pot cover and take a large platter and put it on top of the pot. Flip the pot upside down on the platter. Remove the top parchment paper and enjoy the biryani with tourshi.

## Mom's Biryani (Jean Yonan's Biryani)

2 cups Basmati Rice
4 chicken breasts cut up bite size
1 pound lean ground beef
1 minced onion
4 medium size potatoes peeled, washed cut up bite size
4 hard boiled eggs, peeled and sliced
4 sliced onions
1/2 cup almonds
1/2 cup golden raisins
4 tablespoons Biryani spice
1/2 teaspoon Turmeric
1 tablespoon curry powder
2 tablespoons salt
1/2 teaspoon black pepper
1/3 cup oil
5 cups water
10 cloves crushed garlic
1 cup yogurt

Step 1-Cut up chicken breast bite size and place in a bowl. Sprinkle with 1/2 teaspoon salt and half of the crushed garlic and mix well. Add 1/2 teaspoon turmeric and 1 cup plain yogurt and mix well. Cover and refrigerate for 1 hour.

Step 2-In a bowl, mix 1 pound lean ground beef, 1 minced onion, 1 teaspoon salt, 1 tablespoon biryani spice,1/2 teaspoon black pepper, three cloves crushed garlic. Mix well and form tiny meatballs (the size of marbles).

Step 3-In a large pot add 4 cups of water, 2 tablespoons biryani spice, 1 tablespoon salt, 1 teaspoon turmeric, 1 tablespoon curry powder. Bring to boil and add the rice. Cover and bring and cook on high heat 8-10 minutes, stirring occasionally so the rice doesn't stick to the bottom of pot. When most of the water is evaporated, reduce heat to low and let the rice simmer 30-40 minutes. I usually put a tin under the pot so the rice doesn't stick or scorch.

Step 4-While the rice is cooking, In a large frying pan add 1/2 cup of oil and heat on high. To the hot oil add 1/2 cup almonds and 1/2 cup golden raisins and stir fry 5 minutes. Remove and set aside. To the remaining oil add the cut up potatoes and 1/2 teaspoon salt. Fry till golden on both sides. Remove the potatoes from the oil and set aside. To the remaining oil, add meatballs and fry on all sides, 5 minutes total. Remove the meatballs and set aside. To the remaining oil, add the sliced onions and fry until golden. Reduce heat and let the onions caramelize. Remove onions and lay on top of the fried potatoes and meatballs. To the remaining oil add the marinated chicken, 1 tablespoon Biryani spice, 1/2 teaspoon black pepper, the rest of the crushed garlic and sauté till the chicken is no longer pink. Mix 1 tablespoon tomato paste in a cup of water and add to the chicken. Mix well and sauté 2-3 minutes. Add the fried potatoes, the fried meatballs, and the fried onions to the chicken pan and stir well, combining all ingredients. Let simmer on low 5-7 minutes.

Step 5-When the rice is done, combine the meat pan with the rice pot and mix well. Simmer on low 10 minutes.

Serve the Biryani on a large platter. Spread the almond and raisin mixture over the Biryani. Layer the edges of the Biryani platter with sliced hard boiled eggs.

Enjoy with a side of Assyrian chopped salad and a side of tourshi

## Rizza Zardeh-Assyrian Yellow Rice (Stove top)

3 cups long grain rice or Basmati rice
3 chicken breasts cut up bite size
2 minced onions
5 cloves crushed garlic
5 cups chicken broth
1 cup peas
1 cup diced carrots
1 teaspoon turmeric
1 tablespoon baharat
1/2 teaspoon salt
1 teaspoon cumin powder
1/2 cup oil

Step 1-In a large pot, add 1/2 cup of oil and heat on high. Add the cut up chicken and sauté until no longer pink. Add the onions and sauté 3-5 minutes. Add the Turmeric, baharat and cumin powder and sauté 1-2 minutes. Add the peas and carrots and sauté 2-3 minutes. Add the rice and sauté 2-3 minutes. Add 5 cups of broth and 1/2 teaspoon salt and mix well. Cover and bring to boil, stirring occasionally so the rice doesn't stick to bottom of pot. When the liquid is all evaporated, reduce heat and simmer for 30 minutes. Serve with your choice of salad.

**Rizza d'Shibbit** (Assyrian rice with Fava Beans with Dill)

Preheat oven 350 degrees Fahrenheit

3 cups Basmati rice boiled 8 minutes and strained in a colander
1 large bunch or 2 small bunches of dill de-stemmed, washed, strained, and chopped
1 bag of frozen green Fava Beans or broad beans
2 sticks of butter melted
1 piece of Lawasha bread
1/2 teaspoon turmeric
1/4 cup sea salt
Water

Step 1-Fill a large pot with water and 1/4 cup sea salt and bring to boil. Add the rice and bring to boil 8 minutes. Test a few grains and see if they're still firm. Strain the rice in a colander.

Step 2- In a sauce pan or frying pan melt the butter. Add 1/2 teaspoon Turmeric, the dill and frozen beans and stir well. Sauté 2-3 minutes.

Step 3-In a large roasting pan, add 2-3 tablespoons of oil or butter to coat the bottom of the pot. Add one sheet of lawasha and press to the bottom. Spoon a layer of rice over the lawasha. Add broad beans mixture to the layer of rice and mix well. Add a second layer of rice and broad beans mixture and mix well. Add remaining rice and broad beans mixture over it until all the rice and broad beans mixture have been added. Mix well again and cover with parchment paper. Bake the rice in a preheated oven covered and bake 30-40 minutes until rice is fluffy.

Serve with a nice roast or baked chicken or any kind of cooked fish.

**Rizza Smooqa** (Assyrian Red Rice) Vegetarian for soma (fasting)

3 cups Jasmine rice
4 cups water
1 minced onion

1 chopped green pepper ( I use a hot pepper) to make the rice a bit spicy
1/3 cup oil
1 tablespoon paprika
1 teaspoon salt
1 8-oz can tomato sauce

In a large pot heat 1/2 cup oil. Add 1 minced onion and 1 chopped green pepper and sauté 2-3 minutes. Add 1 tablespoon paprika and sauté another 2 minutes. Add unwashed dry rice and sauté 2-3 minutes. Add 1 can tomato sauce and sauté another 2-3 minutes.

Add 4 cups of water and 1 teaspoon salt and stir well. Cover the pot and bring to boil until all liquid is evaporated, stirring occasionally so the rice doesn't stick to the bottom of the pot. When the water is nearly all evaporated, reduce heat and simmer on low for 30 minutes.

Assyrians of Iraq eat this meal on Wednesdays and Fridays for soma (fasting from meat and dairy). They serve this dish with Assyrian chopped salad, (Zaladda). You can serve it with your choice of salad.


**Mom's Pirda-Cracked wheat**.

My mother loves pirda more than rice. She serves it with baked chicken or beef roasts.

2 cups pirda (cracked wheat or Burghal # 4)
1/2 cup vermicelli
4 cups chicken broth
1 teaspoon salt
4 large sliced onions
1/4 cup oil
3 tablespoons oil for frying the onions

Step 1- In a large pot heat 1/4 cup of oil. Add the vermicelli and sauté 3-4 minutes or until brown. Add the pirda and sauté another 2-3 minutes. Add 4 cups of chicken broth and 1 teaspoon salt. Stir, cover and bring to boil. When the liquid is nearly evaporated, reduce heat, and simmer on low for 20 minutes.

Step 2-In a sauce pan, heat 3 tablespoons of oil. Add the sliced onions and sauté for 5 minutes. Reduce heat, cover and simmer the onions on low to caramelize.

When the Pirda is finished cooking, spoon all the caramelized onions over the pirda. Combine well and allow to rest 10 minutes.

Serve with your choice of salad. I like it with Zaladda, Assyrian chopped salad and tourshi.

## Maqlooba (Upside down rice)

Preheat oven at 450 degrees Fahrenheit

1 pound lean beef stew cut up into small thin strips
3 cups Basmati Rice washed and strained
1/2 cup oil
1/2 cup tomato paste
5 cups of water
1 tablespoon Baharat
2 large eggplants
4 sliced potatoes
3 large onions sliced
1 large green pepper
4 large tomatoes

Step 1-In large pot add 4-5 tablespoons oil. Add the tomato paste and Sauté for 3-5 minutes. Add the washed and strained rice and sauté for 8 minutes. Add 5 cups of water, 1 tablespoons salt and stir well, cover and bring to boil. When the liquid is evaporated, turn heat to low and simmer the rice on low for 30 minutes.

Step 2-While the rice is cooking, in a large skillet add 4 tablespoons of oil, the beef stew and brown for 15 minutes. Add 1 tablespoon Baharat spice and mix well. Sauté 2 minutes. Add 1 cup of water and mix well. Bring to boil and immediately turn heat down to low, cover the pot and let simmer on low until meat is tender.

Step 3-Cut up the potatoes, eggplants, the tomatoes, the peppers, the onions in circles. Place on cookie sheets. Sprinkle with salt on both sides. Let stand for 15 minutes until the eggplants have released their juices and no longer bitter. Pat dry the eggplants with paper towel. Sprinkle all vegetables with oil and bake in the oven for 15- 20 minutes.

Step 4 Assembling the Maqlooba-In large baking dish, add half of the cooked rice to the baking dish and press it down. Layer all the onions on top of the rice. Layer all the tomatoes on top of the onions. Layer all the green peppers on top of the tomatoes. Layer all the eggplants on top of the peppers. Layer all the cooked beef on top of the eggplants. Layer remaining cooked rice on top of the beef. Place parchment paper on top of the meat and press. Cover the pot and bake in the oven for 25 minutes. Remove the pan cover and place a large platter over the pan. Flip the pan upside down gently and remove it slowly.

Maqlooba is complete with rice, meat and vegetables and no side dish is necessary. Serve with the salad of your choice.

## Assyrian Fancy Rice

Preheat oven to 400 degrees Fahrenheit

2 cups Basmati rice washed and soaked 20 minutes
2 julienned carrots
1/4 cup orange peel cut in 1/2 inch strips and soaked and rinsed twice
1/2 cup cranberries
1/2 cup any kind of raisins on hand but best to use golden raisins
1/2 cup slivered almonds
1/2 cup pistachios
1/4 cup milk
1/2 teaspoon ground saffron
1 stick butter
1/4 teaspoon ground cardamom
1/4 teaspoon ground cumin
1/4 teaspoon ground cinnamon
3 cups water
1 tablespoon salt
1/4 cup sugar dissolved in 1/4 cup water

In a small bowl combine the saffron and warm milk and set aside to marinade.

In a small saucepan dissolve 1/4 cup sugar in 1/4 cup water. Add the rinsed orange peel and bring to boil 3-4 minutes. Strain and discard the syrup.

In a large pot, melt butter. Add cardamom, cumin, and cinnamon and sauté 1-2 minutes. Add the nuts, raisins, carrots and cranberries and sauté 2-3 minutes. Add the sugared orange peel and sauté 1-2 minutes. Add the Saffron milk and stir well and boil 2 minutes. Add strained rice and sauté another 2 minutes. Add 3 cups of water, the salt and cover the pot and bring to boil. Uncover and stir twice until you see most liquid is evaporated. Place the rice pot in a preheated oven at 400 degrees Fahrenheit for 10-15 minutes.

Serve with baked chicken or roast

**Rizza Smooqa d'Bisra** (Assyrian red rice with meat)

1 pound beef stew cut up bite size
2 cups Basmati rice washed and strained in a colander
2 minced onions
4 cups water
3 diced Roma tomatoes
6- 8 ounces tomato puree or 3 tablespoons tomato paste.
1 diced green pepper
1 tablespoon salt
1 tablespoon paprika
1/2 cup oil

Step 1-In a large pot heat 2 tablespoons oil and add the cut up beef stew and 1 minced onion. Sauté till the meat is brown. Add 4 cups water, 1 tablespoon salt and bring to boil. Turn down heat and simmer the meat on low until tender, (about 1 hour). Make sure you have at least 3 cups of liquid left and the meat is tender before you start adding the rice.

Step 2-When meat is cooked, drain the liquid broth in a bowl and reserve. To the meat pot add the rest of the oil and heat on high. Add 1 diced onion, 1 diced green pepper and sauté 2-3 minutes. Add 1 teaspoon paprika and sauté 1 minute. Add 3 diced tomatoes and sauté 2-3 minutes. Add tomato puree or paste and sauté 2-3 minutes. Add 2 cups of washed and strained rice, three cups of the reserved beef broth and stir. Bring to boil covered, stirring occasionally so the rice doesn't stick to the bottom of the pot. When all the liquid is nearly evaporated, turn down the heat to low and simmer 40 minutes. Let stand 10 minutes before serving.

Serve with your choice of salad, gillaleh and tourshi

**Rizza d'Parda** (Draped Rice Pie)

This rice dish is wrapped in dough and baked in the oven. But today we make it with ready made Fillo Dough, instead of wasting hours making thin layers of dough.

1 pound cut up Beef Stew meat
2 cups long grain rice, washed and strained
2 minced onions
5 cloves crushed garlic
2 cups peas and carrots (can be frozen)
1 cup slivered almonds
1 cup golden raisins
1 tablespoon Baharat
1 tablespoon curry powder
2 tablespoons salt
1 tablespoon paprika
1 tablespoon black pepper
3 sticks of butter
4 cups water
1 package Fillo Dough


The Stuffing

Step 1-In a large pot heat 3 tablespoons butter and add the cut up beef stew and sauté till the meat is brown. Add 1 minced onion, the crushed garlic and sauté 2-3 minutes. Add 1 tablespoon Baharat, 1 tablespoon salt and sauté 2-3 minutes. Add 2 cups of water, and bring to boil. Turn down heat, cover the pot and simmer on low until meat is tender, about 30-40 minutes.

Step 2-while meat is cooking, in a big pot, melt 1 1/2 sticks butter. Add the slivered almonds and the raisins and fry till the almonds are golden. Remove from the pot and set aside.To the remaining hot butter, add 1 minced onion and sauté 2-3 minutes. Add the peas and carrots and sauté 5 minutes. Add the paprika, the black pepper, and curry powder and sauté 2 minutes. Add the rice and sauté 5 minutes. Add 3 cups of water, 1 tablespoon salt and bring to boil. When most of the liquid is evaporated, turn heat down and simmer on low for 40 minutes.

Step 3-When the rice and meat are cooked, combine both pots in a roasting pan. Add the fried almonds and golden raisins and mix everything to combine.

PREHEAT OVEN 420 DEGREES FARENHEIT

The draping and wrapping

Step 4-Brush the entire roasting pan, including sides with oil, especially the bottom. Take one layer of Fillo dough and put into the pot. Do not cut off the edges that don't fit into the pan. Brush with melted butter, including the edges. Place six layers of buttered Fillo dough into the pan. Add all the rice and meat mixture into the pot. Wrap the edges of the Fillo dough onto the rice, covering and draping it completely. Butter 4 more layers of Fillo dough and place on top of the folded Fillo, tucking the edges inside the pan. Cover the pan and bake for 25 minutes.

Place a platter over the roasting pan. Turn the pan upside down and gently place the pie in the dish. With a knife, cut the sides of the Fillo so that your guests can spoon rice and crispy Fillo to the dish.

Serve with a nice salad of your choice.

## ASSYRIAN KUBBAS -Meat Pies

Kubba started in northern Assyria, Nineveh, to be exact, today's Mosul, and spread to the Arab world.

Many scholars have written about the Assyrian origins of kubba, and from the translated Assyrian tablets we know the word Assyrians used for Kubba was Kubbusu.

Here's another tidbit about Kubbas (meat pies):

"The source for the earliest meat pie recipe comes from ancient Mesopotamia; specifically, from tablets dating to 1700 BC, which were only translated from ancient Assyrian by French academic and chef Jean Bottero in 1985."

This knowledge comes to us from translated clay tablets currently held by Yale University

This is a dough made with either rice and meat or Bulgur and meat, then stuffed with meat, herbs, spices then either boiled, fried, or cooked in sauce as a dumpling. The kubbas that we fry, bake or boil are the bulgur dough kubba. The kubba that is made as a dumpling in sauce or sometimes fried as in kubba d'Halab, is made with rice. There are a variety of kubba shapes, sizes and flavors in the Assyrian tradition.

The Kubba dishes I introduce in this book are strictly Assyrian from today's Iraq and my mother's recipes.

My mother made outrageously good kubbas having lived in Assyria most of her adult life. She raised 4 children while my dad worked and still managed to make these kubbas on a weekly basis. She froze nothing. She made them fresh and served them fresh. But kubbas can be frozen and either fried later, or made and fried then frozen.

As a single mom most of my life, I made both fresh and frozen kubbas, depending on my work schedule. I worked as a full time teacher, as a part-time political activist and as a full-time mom. My life was full, therefore whenever I had extra time, I made kubbas. I cooked half of them and served them fresh, and froze the other half for when I needed a quick meal.

## Kubba d'Mosul-Kubba Pie

The Stuffing
1 pound extra lean ground beef
1 minced onion
5 cloves crushed garlic
2 tablespoons Kubba spice or Baharat (7 spices or Gram Masala)
2 tablespoons oil
1/2 teaspoon salt

Step 1-To a frying pan add 2 tablespoons of oil to coat. Add minced onion and sauté till soft. Add ground beef and sauté till beef is cooked but not too dry. Add the garlic and the seasonings and mix well and sauté for 2-3 minutes. Set aside to cool.

The Dough

2 cups fine bulgur #1 (jreesha) soaked 30 minutes
2 cups extra lean ground beef
1 teaspoon baharat
1/2 teaspoon salt
2 cloves crushed garlic

Step 2-Squeeze out all the water from the burghal and place in a large bowl. Add the ground beef, the garlic, salt and baharat and mix well. Gradually, sprinkle some ice water to make it into a pasty dough, but not too wet and sticky.

On a large cookie sheet, place some plastic wrap and set it aside. On a clean surface, sprinkle some water. Put plastic wrap over the water. Take a pinch of dough and with your hands spread it on the plastic. Place another plastic piece over the opened dough. Sprinkle with water. With a rolling pin, spread out the dough evenly into a large circle the size of a plate. Spoon the stuffing all over the dough leaving a 1/4 inch space around the edges of the dough. Take another pinch of dough and open it the same way you did the first, (between two plastic sheets sprinkled with water). With the rolling pin open the dough and place it over the filling. Seal the edges of the dough, with your wet hands and smooth it out. Gather the plastic wrap and place each finished kubba on the cookie sheet lined with plastic.

In a large pot filled with water, add salt and bring to boil. Very carefully take each kubba and place it in the boiling water for 1 minute, maximum 2 minutes. Remember you're only blanching the kubba, not boiling it. Remove kubba and place it on a plate. Most people eat the kubba this way, blanched, but I like to blanch it first, then fry it in a bit of oil.

Serve with Ambba (pickled mangoes) and enjoy

If this process is too difficult for you, make it into a pan kubba. If you do make the pan kubba, take half the dough and using the plastic and sprinkled water technique open the dough into the shape of your pan. Place dough into the pan, making sure it covers the entire pan. Place all the filling on the dough in the pan. Take the other half of the dough and open it in the same way and place it over the stuffing. With wet hands, smooth the top dough and make sure all the edges are smoothly evened out. Cut the kubba into square or diamond shapes. Brush oil on the dough. Bake in preheated oven at 350 for 30-40 minutes or until top is golden brown.

Serve as main dish or appetizer with tourshi

**Fried Kubba d'Burghal** (jreesh-greesa)

The Dumpling dough

1 pound extra lean ground beef 97% or more
1 cup fine Burghal # 1 soaked for 20 minutes.
3 cloves crushed garlic
1/4 teaspoon salt
1/4 teaspoon black pepper
1 tablespoon baharat

Strain the bulgur and squeeze all excess water. Combine all ingredients and mix well with your hands. Begin to add cold water and work into a dough that's supple but not sticky. Test the dough with your hands and see if it forms a ball. Cover and refrigerate for at least 30 minutes.

The stuffing

1 pound extra lean ground beef 97% or more lean
1 large minced onion
5 cloves crushed garlic
2 tablespoons Baharat
1/2 teaspoon salt
2 tablespoons oil to coat the saucepan.

In a saucepan over medium heat add 2 tablespoons oil to coat the pan. Add the ground beef and brown, breaking it down with a wooden spoon. Add 1 minced onion and sauté 2-3 minutes. Add salt, garlic and Baharat and sauté 2-3 minutes. Cover and set aside to cool.

When the stuffing is cooled, begin to form the kubbas. Take a pinch of dough and form into a ball (the size of a golf ball). Press your thumb down the center of the ball to form a whole. Keep rotating the dough with your other hand until the hole enlarges. Place two teaspoons of stuffing inside the hole. Begin to close the dough, rotating the stuffed ball in your hands. When the whole is closed, begin to roll the kubba between your two palms until you form the shape of a torpedo. Place the stuffed kubbas on a tray. When all the dough is stuffed, deep fry the kubbas in oil on hight heat. Strain and place on paper towels. Serve as appetizer or enjoy it as a main meal with a salad and some tourshi or Amba (pickled mangoes).

Note-You can freeze the kubbas till you're ready to fry them. When freezing them, you must layer them with plastic in between each layer and store them in a tightly sealed container before freezing.

## Smeed Kubba-(Semolina Kubba)

2 pounds extra lean ground beef
1 cup fine burghal #1 soaked in one cup water.
2 minced onions
1/2 cup smeed, (Semolina)
1/2 cup flour
1 cup ground finely chopped walnuts
1 egg
1 tablespoon tomato paste
1 tablespoon paprika
1 teaspoon cumin powder
1 tablespoon baharat
1 teaspoon salt

The Dough
Soak the burghal first then squeeze all excess water out of it. Add salt, flour, smeed, and 1 egg. Knead into a dough. Add 1 tablespoon tomato paste. Add 1 pound raw lean ground beef. Work into a dough.

The Stuffing
Sauté 1 pound ground beef with onions, baharat, garlic, and paprika. Add tomato paste, and 1 cup water and stir well. Bring to boil until all liquid has evaporated. Add the walnuts and sauté 3-5 minutes. Form the kubbas (see the above fried kubba recipe on how to form the kubbas).

Stuff each kubba with meat filling. Fry in oil till golden brown. Remove from oil and Drain on paper towel. Serve with a salad.

## Kubba d'Halab

1 pound extra lean ground beef
1 minced onion
1 diced potato
1/4 cup chopped parsley
4 cloves crushed garlic
2 tablespoons olive oil
1 teaspoon baharat
1 teaspoon curry powder
1 teaspoon salt
1/2 teaspoon black pepper
1 tablespoon chicken stock powder
1/4 teaspoon turmeric
5 cups water
1 1/2 cup basmati or Jasmine rice
Oil for frying

In a pan, add 2 tablespoons oil and heat on high. Add the ground beef and sauté till brown, breaking it down with a wooden spoon. Add 1 minced onion, 4 cloves crushed garlic, 1/2 teaspoon salt, the chopped parsley, teaspoon curry powder, 1 teaspoon baharat, 1/4 teaspoon black pepper and sauté 2-3 minutes. Remove from heat and allow to cool.

Soak the rice 30 minutes and strain. In a pot add the rice, 1 diced potato, 4 cups of water, 1/4 teaspoon salt, and the powdered broth, the turmeric and mix well. Cook the rice until most of the liquid evaporates. Turn low and steam the rice for an additional 20 minutes, till fluffy.

In a food processor grind the cooked rice, cover with plastic and refrigerate for 30 minutes.

Take a golf ball size rice dough and stick your thumb in the center. Open the hole by rotating the dough in your other hand. Spoon 1-2 teaspoons of stuffing and close the dough, dipping your hands in water occasionally to seal the dough. Rub the kubba between your two palms to achieve the torpedo shape shown in picture. After making all the kubba, fry in some oil. Serve with Salad and Tourshi.

## ASSYRIAN KABOBS

Assyrians can't live without their kabob. But most don't know that kabobs have to be kept simple, with as little OTHER ingredients as possible, otherwise, they won't taste good or authentic. Do not add herbs to any kabob otherwise you'll take away the flavor of the meat.

**Chicken Tikka Kabob**

4 skinless, boneless chicken breasts cubed
6 boneless, skinless, chicken thighs cubed
1 minced onion
6 cloves crushed garlic
1/2 teaspoon turmeric
1/2 teaspoon Saffron oil or Saffron marinaded in hot water
3 tablespoons plain yogurt
1 tablespoon Lemon zest
1/2 teaspoon salt
1/4 cup oil

Step 1-Cut the chicken breasts and thighs into 1 inch cubes and place into bowl with lid. Add the rest of the ingredients to the meat and mix well. Cover the mixture and refrigerate over night or at least 1-2 hours.

Step 2-When ready to grill the meat, take one piece at a time and skewer them on a sheesh as shown in the above picture. Place as many sheeshes on the grill as possible. Grill both sides, turning them occasionally, until chicken is no longer pink but not burned or dry. Place in a pot with cover and keep in a warm oven, not hot oven, till ready to serve.

Serve with rice and some grilled vegetables, lawasha and gillaleh.

NOTE-You can also grill the chicken skewers in the oven, using the broiler.


**Beef Sheesh Kabob**

3 pounds 80% lean ground beef
2 minced onions
1 1/2 tablespoons salt
1 tablespoon black pepper

Step 1-In a bowl with cover, combine all ingredients and mix well with your hands. Cover and refrigerate over night, or at least 1-2 hours.

Step 2-You'll need a bowl of ice water to begin putting the beef on a sheesh. Wet your hands with ice water and take a chunk of the marinated beef and begin to stick it onto the sheesh. Keep the meat as cold as possible while you work each sheesh, otherwise the meat will fall off the sheesh. Spread the meat on the sheesh and squeeze to get it stuck on the sheesh (skewer).

Step 3-Place as many sheeshes of beef kabob on the grill as possible, leaving room to turn occasionally. Grill both sides until meat is cooked but still juicy, not dry. Take each cooked skewer or sheesh and slide the meat off it and place them in a pot with a cover. Keep the covered pot of kabob in a warm oven till ready to serve.

NOTE-If it's too difficult to skewer the ground beef, form long patties of beef with your hands and grill in a grilling basket. You can also grill the kabobs in the oven using the broiler to grill them.

## Beef or lamb Tikka Kabob

1 pound sirloin or filet mignon or lamb, cut up into 1 inch cubes
1 minced onion
1 teaspoon salt
1/2 teaspoon black pepper

In a bowl combine all ingredients and mix well. Refrigerate over night or at least 1-2 hours. Skewer the chunks of meat onto a sheesh and grill, turning them over occasionally. Take off the grill while still juicy but cooked.

## Vegetable Kabob-

I serve grilled vegetables with all kabobs. They not only compliment the dish but add superb flavor and nutrition to your meal. I grill the vegetables first before I grill the kabobs, so I can marinade them while the kabobs are grilling.

4 large or 6 Japanese eggplants
6 Roma tomatoes
7 long sweet green chilis
5 cloves crushed garlic
the juice of 1 lemon
1/4 cup virgin olive oil
1/2 teaspoon salt

Step 1-Wash all vegetables and place them on the grill. Grill the vegetables until their skin splits and tears away. That's when you know they're done. Place all grilled vegetables in a plastic bag and seal the bag. Allow to cool before starting to peel them.

Step 2-When the vegetables have cooled, peel off the skin and cut off all stems. Cut up all peeled vegetables into bit size pieces and place them into a large bowl. Add crushed garlic, lemon, salt, and oil and mix well gently. Cover the Bowl and allow them to marinade until ready to serve with the kabobs.

I make baked rice when I grill kabobs. I serve meat and chicken kabobs, baked rice, vegetable kabob and gilalleh.

**Assyrian Beef Guss**-(Guss in Iraqi Arabic means cut)-Shawirma

3 pounds top sirloin sliced
1/4 cup HP sauce or white vinegar
1/4 cup Guss (shawirma) spice. If not available, use Baharat
1/2 teaspoon salt
1/2 cup lard


In a large bowl, combine sliced sirloin, 1/4 cup vinegar or HP sauce, all the spices, the salt, the lard and mix well. Cover the bowl tightly with lid and refrigerate overnight.

Once the meat is marinated, Cut into short strips. In a wok or large frying pan, add all the marinated meat strips and stir fry until brown but still has liquid, approximately 5-7 minutes. Turn heat down, cover the pan and simmer for 30 minutes. The liquid should have evaporated by now. Uncover and stir well on medium heat until all liquid has dried out.

Serve with rice and a salad of your choice or make it into a sandwich.

To use in a sandwich, you'll need to make the Guss sauce that goes with it.

1/4 cup tamarind sauce
1/2 cup plain yogurt
3 cloves crushed garlic
1/2 teaspoon salt

In a blender combine all ingredients and blend. Serve in a bowl on the table with Samoon for those who want to make a sandwich of guss with garlic sauce.

You can also serve the Guss with rice and salad

## Assyrian Chicken Sheesh Tawooq

2 chicken breasts cut into cubes
1 cup plain yogurt
2 tablespoons olive oil
1 teaspoon cumin powder
the juice of 1 lemon
1 teaspoon salt
1 teaspoon coriander powder
1 teaspoon black pepper
1 teaspoon baharat
1 teaspoon nutmeg
2 teaspoons ground sumac
2 tablespoons za'atar
7 cloves crushed garlic
3 tablespoons freshly grated ginger
1/2 jalapeno grated
3 tablespoons oil
1 tomato cubed
1 red onion cubed
1 white onion cubed
1 sweet green pepper cubed

In a bowl, combine the cubed chicken, yogurt, olive oil, cumin, lemon Juice, salt, coriander, black pepper, allspice, nutmeg, za'atar, garlic, and Ginger. Marinade over night or for at least 2 hours for fast cooking.

Skewer the chicken onto wooden skewers, alternating with red and white onions, red and green peppers, and tomatoes.

In a preheated oven, place the Chicken Shish Kebab and vegetable skewers in greased cookie sheet. Cook for 30 to 35 minutes or until brown on both sides. Of course it is best to grill on fire.

Serve with rice or bread

**Cutleteh**

1 pound ground beef
1 minced onion
4 cloves crushed garlic
1/2 bunch parsley de-stemmed, washed and chopped
1 teaspoon salt
1/2 teaspoon pepper
4 tablespoons bread crumbs

Mix all ingredients in a bowl. Form oval shaped flat meat patties. Fry in 4 tablespoons oil until browned on both sides.

Serve as an appetizer or in a sandwich or as a main dish with Rizza Smooqa and zaladda

**Assyrian Purpookheena with Masta tooma-**Purslane with yogurt garlic sauce

3 bunches purpookheena (Purslane) de-stemmed, washed and roughly chopped
1 minced onion
3 cloves crushed garlic
1/4 cup oil
1 tablespoon paprika
1 teaspoon salt
1/2 teaspoon black pepper
1 8-oz can tomato sauce
1/2 cup water

In a pan add oil and heat on high. Add minced onions and garlic and sauté 3-5 minutes until golden. Add paprika and sauté 1 minute. Add chopped Purslane and sauté 3-5 minutes until tender. Add tomato sauce and sauté 2 minutes. Add water, salt and pepper and stir. Turn heat to low, cover the pan and simmer for 10 minutes.

Serve in individual dishes and add yogurt garlic sauce

## DOLMAS-(Prakheh in Assyrian)

Prakhe or 'Dolma' as it came to be known later, is an ancient Assyrian invention that began with the Assyrians who owned their own vineyards. Most Assyrians who owned their own vineyards made their own wines and raisins as well as cultivated a variety of table grapes. The stuffed grape leaves recipe became popular throughout the Middle East when the Ottoman Turks colonized and ruled Assyria. They began to impose their language on all that lived in Assyria and changed its name to a Turkish name, 'DOLMA', which means 'rolled.' The Pontic Greeks and the Armenians living in the Ottoman empire adopted the name 'dolma', as well. But only Assyrians made three types of dolmas, even now. The Armenians learned to make 'Sarma' from the Turks who took the original Assyrian recipe and modified it to stuffed zucchini. Sarma means stuffed zucchini. No other nation knows how to use herbs in making dolma; not the Arabs, the Turks, the Persians or the Greeks. They copied the idea of dolma but not the taste.

After slaughtering as many Assyrians, Armenians and Pontic Greeks as he could, Mustafa Kamal Ataturk confiscated all the Assyrian vineyards owned by the Assyrians he slaughtered, He inherited 1200 varieties of grapes that Assyrians had cultivated over 3 centuries. He also confiscated all their wine and Arak production facilities.

No other nationality is known for its distinct dolma flavors except the Assyrians, due to the usage of specific herbs for each dolma variety. As I said, Assyrians make a variety of dolmas, each one with its own unique and distinct flavor. Other nationalities do not use these specific herbs in their dolmas, and have never been able to replicate these secret and unique flavors and that's how we know that dolma originated in Assyria/ Mesopotamia.

We also know Assyria was the first to domesticate vineyards and produce grapes and wines, when other nations did not exist at the time. This knowledge comes to us from ancient Assyrian tablets which record recipes for wine and beer-making in Assyria. The only people that could possibly make stuffed grape leaves are those that would have grape leaves from the vine.

Any dolma I make I start shopping for the ingredients the day before. The night before I make dolma, I begin to de-stem all the herbs, wash and strain them in colanders, wrap them in a kitchen towel and refrigerate them till I'm ready to make dolma. The shopping and preparing the herbs takes most of the day, and another day is needed just for making the dolma.

Dolma should be made by family, friends or neighbors. Get your kids involved helping you make dolma, by opening the leaves for you and even learning how to roll the dolma.

## Dolma D'Kalama (Cabbage Dolma)

Step 1-The stuffing

1 large or 2 small-medium sized head of cabbage
1 pound beef stew chopped
2 cups short grain rice soaked 20 minutes.
2 large minced onions
3 medium bunch cilantro, de-stemmed, washed and chopped
1 bunch flat leaf parsley de-stemmed, washed and chopped
1 bunch of Kawar (chives) chopped
1 bunch green onions chopped
10 large cloves crushed garlic
2 tablespoons Baharat (All Spice or 7 spices or gram masala)
2 tablespoons paprika
1 teaspoon black pepper
1 1/2 teaspoon salt
1/2 cup oil
4 tablespoons tomato paste
1 8-oz can tomato sauce.
2 tablespoons tamarind sauce
5 plums
7 cups of water

In a large pot with cover, heat 2 tablespoons oil on high. Add 1 minced onion and sauté 2-3 minutes. Add chopped beef and sauté till brown and juicy. Add 4 cups of water, 1 teaspoon salt, 1/4 teaspoon baharat, and bring to boil. Turn to low and let beef simmer till all liquid is evaporated. To the cooked meat, add 1/4 cup of oil, 1 minced onion, and sauté 2-3 minutes. Add the rest of the baharat, paprika, black pepper, and sauté 1-2 minutes. Add the tomato paste and sauté 2 minutes. Remove from stove and allow to cool.

In a large bowl combine the soaked and strained rice, with the sautéed meat, all the chopped herbs, the crushed garlic, 1/2 teaspoon salt and 1 teaspoon black pepper and mix well. Cover the mixture and set aside.

Step 2-
Fill up a very large pot with water and bring to boil on high heat. Using a coring tool, core out the stem that is in the center holding the cabbage leaves together and hollow it out. Immerse the cabbage into the water any time you want, before, during or after the water reaches boiling point, with the cored stem down. The important thing is to watch carefully because you want to blanch the cabbage only, not boil it. While the cabbage sits in the hot water stem down, it will begin to release the leaves to be removed easier. Remove the cabbage leaves as soon as they blanch. Do not allow the cabbage to boil and lose its ability to be stuffed. The cabbage will fall apart in your hands. Piece by piece remove the cabbage leaves and put on a tray.

Step 3-Using a sharp knife, cut each cabbage leaf into smaller pieces (the size of your palm). Lay the cabbage leaf flat over a hard surface. Place 2 tablespoons of stuffing in the center. Fold the cabbage edges over to the center and fold the head over the fold. Begin to roll the cabbage downwards away from you, until you've nearly achieved a cigar shape. Place a few of the discarded leaves on the bottom of the pot. Place the rolled cabbage in the pot over the leaves. After rolling each cabbage, place them into the pot, building a tightly stacked-up rolled cabbage as shown in the picture. Insert washed and de-stemmed whole plums in between, spreading them throughout the pot.

Step 4-The Sauce

After all the stuffing is gone, and you're finished rolling the cabbage, add 3 cups of boiling water into the now empty stuffing bowl. Whirl the water around so that the water picks up all the stuck-on herbs and spices. I do this to develop more flavor. Now add that water to the pot in which you cooked the meat. Do the same by whirling the same water around to pick-up bits and pieces of caramelized beef. To that water add 4 tablespoons tomato paste, 2 tablespoons home-made tamarind sauce,1 teaspoon salt, 1/2 lemon juice, and 1 8-oz can tomato sauce. Mix well and pour over the stacked rolled cabbage.

Drizzle 1/2 cup oil over the rolled cabbage. Place a plate on the rolled cabbage so it may not move during boiling. Cover the pot and bring to boil (10 minutes). Reduce heat and let simmer on low for 30 minutes. Remove from heat and allow to rest at least 30 minutes before serving. This period is for steaming and this process is called DEM. In Assyrian we say "shooq dolma shaqla dem."

Cabbage Dolma should look like this after cooking. It should taste sweet and sour

## Dolma D'Tarpeh-Stuffed Grape Leaves.

When making this dish I use fresh or frozen grape leaves and Swiss Chard.


The Stuffing

1 pound chopped beef for stew or chuck
2 cups short grain rice, Calrose short grain or Jasmine Rice, soaked 20 minutes
1 large stack of grape leaves
2 bunches Swiss chard washed and the stems cut off
2 minced onions divided
10 cloves crushed garlic
1 large or 2 small bunches Dill, de-stemmed, washed, strained, chopped.
If fresh is not available, use one bunch frozen, or 3 tablespoons
dried dill, (Shibit).
1 bunch flat leaf Parsley de-stemmed, washed, strained and chopped
1 bunch kawar (chives) chopped
1 bunch green onions de-stemmed, washed and chopped
1 teaspoon Baharat (All spice, 7-spices, gram masala)
1 teaspoon black pepper
2 teaspoons salt
2 tablespoons paprika
1/4 teaspoon turmeric
1 8-oz can tomato sauce
2 tablespoons tomato paste
1/2 cup oil
6 beef ribs

Step 1-In a large pot, add 2 tablespoons oil and heat on high. Add 1 minced onion and sauté 2-3 minutes. Add the chopped beef and sauté till brown and juicy. Add the turmeric and sauté 1 minute. Add 4 cups of water, 1 teaspoon salt and bring to boil for 5 minutes. Reduce heat and simmer the beef on low, covered.

Step 2- When all the liquid is evaporated from the simmering meat, add 1/4 cup oil, 1 minced onion and sauté 2-3 minutes. Add all the spices (Baharat, paprika, black pepper) and sauté 2-3 minutes. Add 2 tablespoons tomato paste and sauté 2 minutes. Cover and set aside to cool.

Step 3-In a large bowl combine the strained rice, all the chopped herbs, all the crushed garlic, the cooked meat, 1 teaspoon salt, and 1/4 teaspoon black pepper and mix well. Cover and set aside. Save the empty pot you cooked the meat in to cook dolmas in.

Step 4-Fill a large pot with water and bring to a rolling boil. Turn heat low and begin to blanch the fresh grape leaves and the Swiss chard 1 minute each. I blanch all the fresh grape leaves together for 1 minute and then strain in a colander. Then blanch the Swiss chard bunches together and strain as well.

When the grape leaves and Swiss chard have cooled, you can begin to roll. Before starting to roll the dolma, place the ribs into the pot you cooked the meat in. When you roll the dolma place the first layer of rolled dolmas on top of the ribs.

Lay each grape leaf open on a counter and spoon 2 tablespoons of the stuffing in the top center of the leaf. Fold the edges of the grape leaf to the center, covering the stuffing, and fold the head of the leaf over the folded edges. Begin to roll downwards away from you until you reach the tail end of the leaf. Lay each rolled grape leaf into the pot you cooked the meat in, stacking it over the ribs. After layering all the rolled grape leaves on one side of the pot, begin rolling the Swiss Chard.

Take each piece of Swiss chard and cut it the size of your palm, discarding the stems. Spoon 2 tablespoons of stuffing onto the chard. Fold the edges to the center, covering the stuffing, and fold the head of the chard over the folds. Begin to roll the chard downwards away from you. It should look like a rolled cigar. Place all the rolled Swiss chard into the other side of the pot, stacking them up all the way to the top. See picture below. Leave 3 inches to the top for boiling.

When blanched, the grape leaves will turn a lighter shade of green, whereas the Swiss chard maintains its color.

78

The Sauce

Add three cups of boiling water to your now empty stuffing bowl to pick up all the stuck-on herbs and spice. To that water add 1 can tomato sauce, (except 1 tablespoon to reserve for Kazkazta), and 1 teaspoon salt, 1/4 teaspoon black pepper and stir well. Add the sauce to the pot, and drizzle 1/2 cup of oil over the stacked grape leaves. Place a plate on the dolma so they don't move while boiling. Cover the pot and bring to boil for 10 minutes. Turn heat to low and simmer the dolma for 30 minutes. Remove from heat and let the dolma rest and steam for 30 minutes before serving.


The Toppings-There are two toppings that go on the plated dolma: 1) Masta Tooma ( yogurt garlic sauce) and 2) Kazkazta (Fried onion sauce.)

Masta Tooma-Yogurt garlic sauce
3 cups plain yogurt
4 cloves crushed garlic
Mix well and put into a bowl with lid and refrigerate till use.

Kazkazta-Fried onion sauce
1/4 cup oil
1 large minced onion
1 tablespoon paprika
1 tablespoon tomato sauce

In a saucepan, add 1/4 cup oil, 1 minced onion. Fry for 10-15 minutes. Add the paprika and mix well for 1 minute. Add 1 tablespoon tomato sauce and sauté 2 minutes. Cover and set aside to cool.

The yogurt sauce and the kazkazta go on the table. Place a large tray over the dolma pot and turn the dolma over so that all the dolma spills on to the tray. Dolma is served on a silver platter because it is food of the Gods and therefore divine. Once the dolma is plated in individual servings the person can choose to add Masta Tooma followed by kazkazta or one or the other.

Others might not eat the sauces. Each person has their own palate and different taste. Some people prefer the taste of dolma by itself, without adding layers of flavors to the dolma. Try both.

Below is a picture of Dolma d'Tdarpeh (Stuffed grape leaves) and Silqa (Swiss Chard dolma) served with masta tooma and kazkazta). Once you have been served dolma d'Tdarpeh, and you want it with masta tooma and kazgkzta, you drizzle a few spoonfuls of yogurt sauce over the dolma on your plate, first, then kazkazta over the masta tooma.

Dolma with Masta Tooma and kazkaza

## Dolma d'Rangeh-Seven Mixed Vegetables Colorful Dolma

6 Japanese eggplants, de-stemmed and cut in half width side, making 2 eggplants
4 long sweet green chilis or poblano peppers
6 hot banana peppers
4 Roma tomatoes
1 onion pounded and the layers removed.
4 zucchinis cut in half
1 stack blanched fresh grape leaves, or frozen leaves
1 bunch Swiss chard blanched
1 1/2 pounds of chopped beef stew or chuck,
2 cups short grain rice soaked 20 minutes and strained (Calrose, or Blue Rose)
2 large minced onions
10 cloves crushed garlic
2 bunches de-stemmed, washed and chopped Cilantro.
1 bunch de-stemmed, washed and chopped flat leaf parsley
1 bunch kawar (chives) chopped
1 bunch chopped green onions
3 tablespoons chopped fresh or frozen Talkhoun (Tarragon)
1 tablespoons chopped Iryaneh (basil)
1 chopped hot pepper
1/2 cup oil
2 tablespoons Baharat
1 tablespoon paprika
1 teaspoon salt
1 teaspoon black pepper
2 qooyra ( two clusters of sour grapes) or 1 sour apple quartered
The juice of two lemons
1 8- ounce can tomato paste
1 8-oz can tomato sauce.

Step 1-In a large pot, add 2 tablespoons oil and heat on high. Add 1 minced onion and sauté 2-3 minutes. Add the chopped beef, 1 tablespoon baharat and sauté till brown yet juicy. Add 4 cups of water, 1/4 teaspoon salt and bring to boil for 5 minutes. Reduce heat and simmer the beef on low, covered.

Step 2- When all the liquid is evaporated from the simmering meat, add 1/4 cup oil, 1 minced onion and sauté 2-3 minutes. Add all the spices,1 tablespoon Baharat, paprika, black pepper and sauté 2-3 minutes. Add 2 tablespoons of tomato sauce and 2 tablespoons tomato paste and sauté 2 minutes. Set aside to cool.

Step 3-In a large bowl combine the strained rice, all the chopped herbs, all the crushed garlic, and the cooked meat and mix well. Cover and set aside. Save the empty pot you cooked the meat in to wrap dolmas in.

Step 4-Cut up the eggplants and zucchinis in half. Core all the eggplants and zucchinis with a coring tool. Slit the tops of the tomatoes but do not cut all the way. Core the insides of the tomatoes with a teaspoon and place the cores into the empty meat pot.

Remove the stems from the peppers and take out all the seeds from inside the peppers. Do not discard the stems, only the seeds. You'll be using the stem to seal the pepper after you stuff it. Pound the unpeeled onion against the counter till it is tender. Peel the onion and make an incision into its layer, and begin to separate each layer. De-stem, wash and blanch the Swiss chard. Blanch the fresh grape leaves.

Step 5-When all the vegetables are ready to be stuffed, begin by stuffing some of the large vegetables first and laying them flat into the meat pot, mixing them up so that each layer of dolma contains at least one of the vegetables. Roll some Swiss chard and grape leaves and tuck them between the vegetables, along with a cluster of sour grapes on each end of the pot. If sour grapes are not available, use sour apples. Repeat until all vegetables as well as the grape leaves and Swiss chard are stuffed, making sure it is a tight fit, not loose. The tighter the dolma is layered the better the results. See pictures below for before and after.

The Sauce-After all the stuffing is gone, pour 3 cups of hot water into your empty stuffing bowl and whirl it around so that the water picks up all the stuck-on herbs and spices. To that water add 1 teaspoon salt, the lemon juice, and the remaining tomato sauce. Mix well and pour over the stacked dolma.

Drizzle 1/4 cup oil and the remaining tomato sauce over the dolma. Place a plate on the rolled dolma so it may not move during boiling. Cover the pot and bring to boil (10 minutes). Reduce heat and let simmer on low for 30 minutes. Remove from heat and allow to rest at least 30 minutes before serving. This period is for steaming and this process is called DEM. In Assyrian we say "shooq dolma shaqla dem."

Sauce and oil added to stuffed dolma.

This is how dolma should look after it's cooked. Serve with lawasha and enjoy.

## Vegetarian/Vegan Dolma d'Tarpeh for Soma (fasting)-Stuffed grape leaves and Swiss chard

The Stuffing
1 bag (1 pound) fresh or frozen green Fava Beans roughly chopped
2 cups short grain rice (Calrose or Blue Rose) soaked and strained
2 bunches dill de-stemmed, washed and chopped
1 bunch flat leaf parsley de-stemmed, washed and chopped
1 bunch green onions chopped
1 bunch Kawar (chives) chopped
2 minced onions
10 cloves crushed garlic
1 tablespoon paprika
1 teaspoon turmeric
1 teaspoon salt
1/2 teaspoon black pepper.
1 8-oz can tomato sauce
1/4 cup oil

Wash and soak the rice for 1/2 hour then strain and place into a bowl.

In a saucepan, add 1/4 cup oil and heat on high. Add the minced onions and sauté 2-3 minutes. Add the paprika and turmeric and sauté 2-3 minutes. Add the tomato sauce and sauté 2 minutes. Set aside to cool.

In a large bowl, combine the strained rice, all the chopped herbs, the sautéed onions, the garlic, the chopped Fava beans, salt and pepper and mix well.

Roll the grape leaves and the Swiss chard as shown in the previous pages (Dolma d'Tarpeh). Stack them up in a large pot with lid.

The Sauce
1/4 cup oil
2 tablespoons tomato paste
3 cups water
1 teaspoon salt
1/4 teaspoon black pepper
the juice of half a lemon

In a bowl combine all ingredients and whisk to blend. Pour all over the rolled dolma. Place a plate on the dolma so it doesn't't move during boiling. Cover the pot and bring to boil 10 minutes. Reduce heat and let simmer on low 30 minutes. Remove from heat and let rest 30 minutes. Serve with yogurt and garlic sauce and kazkazta as shown in Dolma d'Tarpeh.

## APPPETIZERS

Appetizers are an important part of Assyrian daily life. They are used as snacks in between meals and are also served as side dishes with main meals or as condiments. Ancient Assyrian tablets attest to the fact appetizers, dips and salsas were made and even relishes and table condiments were served with every meal. "One of the tablets from 1700 B.C. instructs the cook to send these condiments and appetizers to the table accompanied with garlic, greens, and vinegar." Jean Bottero.

Ancient Assyrians also served dips, called 'Sapu' (the variant Saba'u) an Akkadian word which means to soak or drench. This word was adopted by all Mesopotamians including Arabs who later came to live in Assyria and they used it as "Saba" which means to baptize. The word has changed in pronunciation but not the meaning. Those followers of John the Baptist in Northern Iraq are still called Subba, or Subbeans/Sabeans.

In ancient Assyria mustard and vinegar were made into condiments and dips using a bit of oil, chopped parsley, chopped garlic, etc. These were the original salsas.

## Assyrian meat Samboosak

Samboosak are also called Samosas in Hindi. But the Indians of India don't make a meat Samosa. This Samboosak recipe is with meat and it originates in Basra.

I recommend buying wonton skins or Fillo dough to wrap your Samboosak with if you don't have time to make a dough. But if you do want to try this easy dough recipe for Samboosak then I have included it here.

The Dough
2 cups flour
1 teaspoon salt
1/2 teaspoon baking powder
1/4 cup oil
2/3 cup water

You'll also need a bowl of water to wet your hands when forming and shaping the Samboosak.

In a bowl mix the flour, salt, and baking powder and stir well. In another bowl mix the water and oil and stir well. Gradually pour the water/oil mixture into the flour bowl and begin to form the dough, mixing with one hand and pouring with the other until you have formed a smooth consistency. Knead the dough well and cover and allow the dough to rest for 30 minutes.

While the dough is resting, make the filling.

The Filling
1 pound extra lean ground beef
2 large minced onions
1 chopped green Chile. If you like it hot then use a jalapeño
2 tablespoons baharat
1 tablespoon freshly grated ginger
4 cloves crushed garlic
1 teaspoon ground cumin
1 teaspoon ground coriander seeds
1 teaspoon turmeric
1 teaspoon paprika or chili powder
1/2 teaspoon ground cinnamon
1/2 teaspoon ground cardamom
1/2 teaspoon black pepper
1 teaspoon salt
2 tablespoons oil

In a frying pan heat 2 tablespoons oil to coat the pan. Add the ground beef and sauté till brown 3-4 minutes, breaking the beef down with a wooden spoon. Add minced onions, chopped chili pepper, ginger, and garlic and sauté 2-3 minutes till onions are soft. Add the rest of the spices and the salt and sauté 2-3 minutes. Remove from heat and allow the filling to cool.

Cut the dough into 16 equal parts. With a rolling pin open each dough ball into a flat disk. Spoon 2 tablespoons of filling on one side of the disk. Fold over the second side of the disk, wetting your hand to seal the halves. Crimp the seal with your fingers. Repeat until all 16 dough balls have been opened and stuffed and sealed.

Fry or bake the Samboosak and serve as appetizers with Chicken curry or beef curry and rice or a main meal with a nice salad.


Baking the Samboosak

Whip one egg and brush the Samboosak with the egg wash. Sprinkle with Nigella seeds. Bake 25 minutes at 365 degrees Fahrenheit.

**Assyrian Potato Chap**-Stuffed and fried potatoes

The dough

4 large Idaho potatoes boiled and peeled
2 eggs
½ teaspoon salt
1/4 teaspoon turmeric

Place the boiled and peeled potatoes in the food processor and pulse until well mashed. Place it in a bowl and add the salt and 2 beaten eggs. Knead the dough well with your hands and set aside.

The Filling:
1 pound extra lean ground beef
1 large minced onion
5 cloves crushed garlic
1 small bunch flat leaf parsley, de-stemmed, washed and chopped.
½ teaspoon salt
1 teaspoon black pepper
1 tablespoon curry powder
1 cup vegetable oil for frying

Add 2 tablespoons of oil to a frying pan and heat on high. Add the ground beef and brown. Add the minced onions, the parsley, the garlic and all the spices and sauté 2-3 minutes. Set aside to cool.

Take a small piece of potato dough and form into a golf size ball. Press the center with your thumb to form a hole. Place 1 tablespoon of filling into the hole and close it with your hands. Press into a disk shape. Place the patties on a tray and refrigerate for 30 minutes.

Heat oil in the pan and drop in the potato patties. Add more oil as needed. When golden brown, turn to the other side. Drain on paper towel. Serve hot as an appetizer.

## Meat Bourag-Assyrian Egg Rolls

I no longer make a dough for these beauties. I buy Won Ton Wrap or Spring Roll wrap.

The Filling
1 pound extra lean ground beef
1 large minced onion
5 cloves crushed garlic
1 bunch parsley de-stemmed, washed, dried with paper towel & chopped
1/2 teaspoon salt
1/2 teaspoon black pepper
1 1/2 tablespoons Curry Powder
1/2 cup of oil

In a frying pan, add 2 tablespoons of oil and heat on high. Add the ground beef and brown, breaking it down with a wooden spoon. Add minced onions, crushed garlic, chopped parsley, and all the spices and sauté 2-3 minutes. Set aside to cool.

The dough-Spare yourself sometime and hard work and just buy any size won ton skins or spring roll wraps. Lay each wonton skin flat on a board. Place 2 tablespoons of filling in the center of each wonton skin. Pick up the side edges of the won ton skin and bring to center to fold. Wrap the egg roll into a cigar shape.

Heat 1/2 cup of oil on medium heat. Place 5 egg rolls at a time into the hot oil and fry until golden brown on all sides. Drain on paper towel and serve with any pickle, especially Assyrian pickles.

## A'aroug-Meat and vegetable patty

2 pounds ground beef or ground chicken or ground turkey
1 bunch green onions cleaned, washed and chopped
1 green sweet pepper chopped
1 bunch parsley de-stemmed, washed and chopped
2 tomatoes chopped
2 tablespoons fresh mint chopped
5 cloves crushed garlic
2 cups flour
1 cup fine #1 Bulgar soaked and drained
2 teaspoons baking powder
3 eggs
2 tablespoons curry powder
1/2 teaspoon black pepper
1/2 teaspoon salt
1/2 teaspoon turmeric
1/2 teaspoon paprika
1 1/2 cups water
1 cup oil for frying

In a large bowl mix the flour and the drained and squeezed bulgar. Beat the eggs and add to mixture. Mix well. Add the ground beef and mix well. Add all the chopped vegetables, the garlic, the spices, herbs and the water and begin mixing with your hands. Cover the bowl with plastic wrap and refrigerate for an hour.

Heat one cup of oil in a frying pan. Take a spoonful of mixture and add to the hot oil. With the spoon flatten the mixture and fry on both sides till golden brown.

Drain on paper towels and serve as appetizer.

You can also serve the A'aroug as a main meal with salad. It is very filling.

**Laham Ajeen**

2 pounds ground beef
2 minced onions
10 cloves crushed garlic
1 bunch flat leaf parsley de-stemmed, washed, chopped
1/2 8-oz can tomato paste
1 teaspoon salt
1 teaspoon black pepper
1 tablespoon paprika
1 package flour tortillas or 1 package pizza dough, or make your own dough if you want.

Preheat oven 350 degrees Fahrenheit

In a large bowl combine ground beef, and remaining ingredients and mix well. Take a tortilla and spread some of the meat mixture all over it. Put on cookie sheet and bake until edges of tortilla are golden brown. Repeat until you've used all the meat mixture. Serve with a salad.

## Hummus

1 12- oz can Garbanzo beans
4 cloves crushed garlic
the juice of 2 lemons
7 tablespoons or 1/2 cup Tahini (Takhin)
1/4 cup virgin olive oil
1 teaspoon salt

Mix the Tahini jar well to blend the oil and paste. In a food processor, grind the garlic.
Pour 7 tablespoons of tahini, and the juice of 2 lemons and process on high.

Tahini will thicken slightly. In a bowl empty the contents of the can of garbanzo beans.
With a slotted spoon strain the garbanzo beans and add them to the food processor.
Add 2 tablespoons of the garbanzo juice and the olive oil to the food processor. Process
until the mixture is creamy and smooth. Add the salt and process again.

Serve in a deep dish and drizzle with some extra virgin olive oil and if you like heat,
sprinkle with a pinch of cayenne pepper. I also decorate the hummus either with olives
or moukhalalat.

Enjoy with pita bread or lawasha, or pita chips

## Baba Ghanouj

4 eggplants roasted.
2 tablespoons plain yogurt
4 tablespoons Tahini
2 cloves crushed garlic
the juice of 1 lemon
1/4 teaspoon salt

Wash and roast the eggplants in the oven or on a grill until their skin splits which means it is done. Place in a plastic bag while hot and seal the bag. Allow the eggplants to cool to make it easier to peel off the skin. After peeling off the skin and cutting off the stems, place the peeled eggplants into food processor and pulse until it is a chunky blend, but not too smooth. Place the eggplants in a bowl and add 2 cloves of crushed garlic, 2 tablespoons yogurt, 4 tablespoons of Tahini, 1/4 teaspoon salt, and the juice of 1 lemon. Mix well and serve in a dish.

Drizzle with extra virgin olive oil before serving. If you like heat sprinkle with a pinch of cayenne. Enjoy with pita bread or lawasha.

## Foul M'Dammaz

2 cans Fava Beans
4 cloves crushed garlic
3 tablespoons lemon juice
1/4 teaspoon salt
1 chopped tomato
3 chopped green onions

Heat two cans of Fava Beans in a saucepan with the juice. Bring to boil. Add
2 cloves crushed garlic, 3 tablespoons lemon juice and 1/4 teaspoon salt.
Mash the beans with a fork until chunky but no longer whole. Serve in a dish. Drizzle
with olive oil. Place chopped green onions in the middle of the bowl. Place chopped
tomatoes around the green onions.

Enjoy with pita bread or lawasha.

## Baked Spinach Bourag

2 bunches or 2 bags of fresh spinach
1 large minced onion
2 cloves crushed garlic
1/4 cup oil
1/4 teaspoon salt
1/4 teaspoon mild black pepper
1 cup shredded Monterey Jack cheese or Bulgarian Fetta cheese.
1 package of puff pastry

In a frying pan add the oil and heat on high. Add the minced onion and sauté 2-3 minutes. Add the crushed garlic and sauté 1 minute. Add the spinach and sauté 3-5 minutes. Add the salt and black pepper and stir. Let the liquid evaporate before removing from heat. Remove from heat and allow to cool. When the Spinach is cooled, add the cheese and mix well.

Preheat oven at 350 degrees Fahrenheit

Open the puff pastry package and lay flat on the cutting board. Slice the pastry sheet into 4x4 pieces. Spoon 2-3 tablespoons of spinach mixture on one side of each slice. Fold the other side over the spinach mixture. Seal the dough with your fingers.

Place each stuffed spinach Bourag on a cookie sheet. Bake for 15-20 minutes or until golden brown. Enjoy with a salad.

**Falafel**
1 cup dry chickpeas (khardamaneh) soaked overnight and strained
1/2 can Fava Beans (Bagela) strained
1 minced onion
3 cloves crushed garlic
1 teaspoon baking powder
1 cup de-stemmed, washed, and chopped parsley
1 teaspoon baking soda
1 teaspoon ground coriander seeds
1 teaspoon cumin powder
1 teaspoon salt
1/2 teaspoon black pepper
Oil for frying

In a food processor grind the strained chickpeas and place in a large bowl. Grind the Fava Beans in the same processor and add to the bowl. Grind the garlic in the processor and add the chopped parsley, the minced onion to it and grind together in the same food processor. Add all ingredients and mix well in the bowl forming a pasty dough.

Pinch a chunk of the dough and form golf size balls. Press lightly into a patty. Place on parchment paper. Heat oil on high and deep fry the falafel balls till golden brown on all sides. Set on paper towel to drain the oil.

Tahini Sauce

1/4 cup Tahini
3 cloves crushed garlic
4 tablespoons extra virgin olive oil
1/4 cup lemon juice
warm water
Salt to taste

In a bowl combine tahini, garlic, lemon juice and olive oil and stir well. Gradually add some warm water and stir constantly until you reach the consistency of a creamy salad dressing. Salt to taste.

Falafel Sandwich

Make a slit into a pita bread or Samoon. Stuff with falafel, sliced tomatoes, and drizzle with Tahini Sauce

You don't have to eat the falafel in a sandwich. They make great appetizers. Place the fried falafel in a platter. Pour the Tahini sauce in a small bowl and place it in the center of the platter. Serve as appetizer, where you can dip the falafel into the Tahini sauce and enjoy.

**Masta Khyareh-Assyrian Yogurt Cucumber and Dill Dip**

2 cups plain yogurt whipped with a fork
2 peeled and chopped cucumbers
1/2 bunch fresh dill de-stemmed, washed and chopped
1/4 teaspoon salt

In a bowl add the yogurt and beat with a fork until smooth. Add chopped cucumbers and dill and mix well. Add 1/4 teaspoon salt and mix well. Refrigerate and serve chilled.

Serve will lawasha, Samoon or Pita chips

## ASSYRIAN SOUPS

### Assyrian Chicken and Rice soup

3 chicken breasts chopped
1/2 cup rice soaked for 30 minutes, then strained.
1/2 bag frozen okra chopped
1 zucchini washed and chopped
10 cups water
1/2 bunch flat leaf parsley de-stemmed, washed and chopped
1 minced onion
1 poblano pepper washed and chopped or any green pepper you like.
1 tablespoon paprika
1/2 teaspoon black pepper
1 8-oz can tomato sauce
1/4 cup oil

In a large pot heat the oil and add the chopped chicken. Sauté the chicken until no longer pink. Add the minced onion and chopped green pepper and sauté 3-4 minutes. Add the paprika and sauté 1 minute. Add the rice, zucchini and okra and sauté 2-3 minutes. Add the water and tomato sauce and stir well. Add the chopped parley and bring mixture to a boil. Add salt and pepper to taste. After boiling 10 minutes, reduce heat to low and simmer covered for 30 minutes. Allow to rest for 10 minutes before serving.

Serve with Samoon or baguette.

### Tashrib with Spinach Soup

10 chicken drumsticks
1 bag spinach
1 can garbanzo beans strained
4 cups chicken broth
1 minced onion
1 cup flour
1 tablespoon Turmeric
1 tablespoon cumin powder
1 tablespoon ground cilantro seeds
4 cloves crushed garlic
1 tablespoon kosher salt or coarse sea salt
4 tablespoons oil

In a bowl salt the chicken pieces. In another bowl with 1 cup flour, dunk the chicken in flour and coat well. Set aside.

In a large pan add 4 tablespoons oil and heat on high. Fry the chicken on both sides. Do not cook through. Set aside to cool.

To the oil pot add 1 minced onion and sauté 2-3 minutes. Add all the spices and sauté 2-3 minutes. Add 4 cups of chicken broth and stir well. Return the fried chicken back into the broth pot. Add the garbanzo beans and stir well. Bring to boil for 2 minutes.

Cover the pot and cook in a preheated oven at 400 degrees Fahrenheit for 1 hour. Take out of the oven and add the spinach. Stir well to combine. Cook 10 minutes on stove top until the spinach is tender. Allow to cool for 10 minutes before serving.

This is a very hearty soup that you can eat with bread.

You can substitute drumsticks for any chicken parts. I prefer this dish with chicken breasts. I use six chicken breasts cut up, salted, then covered in flour and fried. Then follow the recipe.


## Assyrian Chicken Noodle Soup

3 large chicken breasts chopped
1 minced onion
2 cloves crushed garlic
1 cup thin noodles or vermicelli
1/2 bunch flat leaf parsley de-stemmed, washed and chopped
1 cup frozen peas and carrots
6 cups water
2 tablespoons chicken bouillon
1/4 teaspoon turmeric
1/4 cup oil
Salt and pepper to taste

In a large soup pot heat 1/4 cup oil on high. Add the chopped chicken breasts and sauté until no longer pink. Add the minced onion and garlic and sauté 2-3 minutes. Add the turmeric and the thin noodles and sauté 1 minute. Add the frozen vegetables and sauté 2-3 minutes. Add the water, parsley and bouillon and stir well to combine. Bring to boil 5 minutes. Reduce heat and simmer on low for 30 minutes. Before adding salt, taste the soup because the bouillon is salty. Add salt and pepper to taste.

Serve with your favorite bread

## Assyrian Red Lentil Soup

1 cup red lentils washed and strained
1 minced onion
2 cloves crushed garlic
1 tablespoon chopped parsley
1 teaspoon curry powder
1/2 teaspoon turmeric
1/2 cup Vermicelli
4 tablespoons oil
5 cups water
1 teaspoon salt

In a large pot add the oil and heat on high. Add the minced onion and sauté 3-5 minutes until golden. Add the turmeric and curry and sauté another 2-3 minutes. Add the Vermicelli and sauté another 2-3 minutes. Add the lentils and garlic and sauté another minute. Add the water, parsley, salt and stir well. Bring to boil. Reduce heat and allow the lentils to cook, stirring occasionally until they're creamy.

Serve hot in a bowl with Samoon

## Assyrian green lentil soup

2 cups green lentils
1 minced onion
4 cloves crushed garlic
3 carrots chopped
3 stalks of celery chopped
1/2 bunch cilantro chopped
The juice of 1 lemon
1 tablespoon paprika
1 teaspoon turmeric
1 teaspoon cumin
1 teaspoon salt
1/2 teaspoon black pepper
2 tablespoons tomato paste
1 tablespoon dry mint
6 cups water
2 tablespoons oil

In a large pot heat 2 tablespoons oil. Add minced onion and sauté 2-3 minutes. Add the paprika and sauté 1 minute. Add the turmeric and cumin and sauté 1 minute. Add the lentils and sauté 2-3 minutes. Add the garlic, carrots, celery, and sauté 2 minutes. Add the tomato paste and sauté 2 minutes. Add the water, mint, salt and pepper and bring to boil.

Turn heat low and cover the pot. Simmer for 1 hour. When the lentils are soft, it is done. Remove from heat and add the juice of 1 lemon. Serve in individual bowls.

Serve with your favorite bread and salad

**Assyrian Beef Barley Soup**

1 1/2 pounds beef stew chopped and a few soup bones
1 cup pearled barley
1/2 bunch flat leaf parsley de-stemmed, washed and chopped
1 bunch green onions chopped
2 minced onions
4 cloves crushed garlic
4 stalks celery chopped
6 carrots chopped
3 tablespoons oil
6 cups water
3 cans beef broth
1 tablespoon paprika
1 1/2 teaspoon salt
3 tablespoons tomato paste
1/2 teaspoon black pepper

In a large pot heat 3 tablespoons of oil on high. Add chopped meat and sauté until brown. Add 2 minced onions and the garlic and sauté 5 minutes. Add the tomato paste and sauté 2 minutes. Add the barley and sauté 1 minute. Add the carrots, celery and parsley and sauté 2-3 minutes. Add 6 cups of water, 3 cans of beef broth, the chopped green onion, salt and pepper and bring to boil for 15 minutes. Reduce heat and simmer for 3 hours, stirring occasionally.  Serve with your favorite bread.

## Assyrian Soup d'Lehana/Kalama

1 cabbage sliced
1 1/2 pounds of meat with bone (any kind you prefer lamb, or beef)
1 cup yellow split peas soaked for an hour then strained
1 minced onion
1 tablespoon turmeric
1 bay leaf
1 teaspoon ground coriander seeds
1 teaspoon cumin powder
1/2 teaspoon black pepper
1 tablespoon paprika
1 tablespoon salt
1 8-oz can tomato sauce
2 tablespoons oil
Water

In a large pot add the oil and heat on high. Add the minced onion and sauté 2-3 minutes. Add the meat with bone, cumin powder, coriander powder, black pepper and brown the meat on all sides. Add paprika and turmeric, and sauté 1 minute. Add the tomato sauce and sauté 2 minutes. Add the split peas and sauté 2 minutes. Fill the pot 3/4 of the way with water. Leave 3-4 inches space to the top of the pot for boiling. Bring the pot to boil. Reduce heat and let the meat simmer for 1 hour till tender.

Add the sliced cabbage and 1 bay leaf and stir well to combine. Bring the pot to boil again. Reduce heat and let simmer for 20 minutes.

Serve into individual bowls with your favorite bread.


**FOR YOGURT BASED SOUPS REFER TO ASSYRIAN MILK PRODUCTS SECTION.

# ASSYRIAN MILK PRODUCTS

## ASSYRIAN MASTA-YOGURT

Assyrians cannot live without their yogurt. It's always on the table to be eaten with something. We also use yogurt to make soups, salads, sauces, dips, drinks, even baked goods. It is one of the most important appetizers, which is why I have placed it under Assyrian Milk Products, as well as in the appetizer section. Many Assyrians will serve Masta with any rice dish.

## Masta-Yogurt

1/2 gallon whole milk
1 cup cream
1/4 cup plain yogurt for culture

In a large pot combine milk and cream and stir well. Bring to boil. Remove from heat and allow to cool a few minutes. It should be still hot to the touch but not burning, that's when you know it's ready to be cultured. Add 1/2 cup plain yogurt (culture) and stir well. Cover the bowl with plastic then a heavy blanket and store in a warm space overnight. In the morning you will have the most delicious MASTA, yogurt.

## Boushala-Assyrian yogurt soup with herbs

8 cups yogurt
1 egg
2 tablespoons flour
1 bunch Cilantro de-stemmed, washed and chopped.
5 stalks of celery washed and chopped
1/2 bunch dill de-stemmed, washed and chopped,
1/2 bunch mint washed and chopped or 2 tablespoons dried mint
1 bunch purslane washed and chopped
3 hot peppers
1/2 cup barley soaked overnight
10 cups water
Salt to taste

In a large pot, mix plain yogurt, the egg and the flour with a hand mixer until smoothly blended. Add the water and the barley and mix well. On medium heat stir the pot constantly and bring to boil. Do not stop even for a second otherwise the yogurt will curdle. Once the mixture boils add the herbs one at a time and the celery, stirring constantly. Add the hot peppers and keep stirring. When the celery becomes tender turn off stove. Add salt to taste.

Do not add salt until you have removed the pot from heat.

Some Assyrians use chopped spinach or chopped Swiss chard when there's no purslane (purpokheena) available.

Serve with lawasha

## Creamy Chicken and Rice soup

2 chicken breasts chopped
1/2 cup diced carrots
1/2 cup diced celery
1 minced onion
2 tablespoons oil
2 cups milk
2 cups chicken broth
1/2  cup Calrose short grain rice or Jasmine rice
2 tablespoons flour
Salt and pepper to taste
1 cup water

In a large pot, heat 2 tablespoons oil. Add minced onions, celery, carrots and sauté 2-3 minutes. Add the chicken and sauté 3-4 minutes. Add flour and sauté 2-3 minutes. Add the rice and sauté 2 minutes. Add the chicken broth and milk and stir to combine. Add 1 cup water and bring the pot to boil. Simmer for 30-40 minutes until rice is soft and creamy. Add salt and pepper to taste at the end, because the broth sometimes can be salty.

Serve in a bowl with Samoon or your favorite bread.

## Yogurt with meatballs soup

The meatballs

2 pounds ground beef
1 minced onion
1/2 cup rice, soaked, strained and ground
6 cups yogurt
1 egg
2 tablespoons flour
2 cups beef broth
1/4 cup chopped parsley
4 cloves crushed garlic
1 can garbanzo beans strained
1/2 cup cooked rice
1 tablespoon mint
1 teaspoon dill
4 cloves crushed garlic
1 teaspoon salt
1 teaspoon black pepper

In a big bowl combine ground beef, the ground rice, 1 minced onion, garlic, and 1 teaspoon salt, 1 teaspoon black pepper. Mix well. Start forming small meatballs the size of golf balls.

The sauce
In a large pot add all yogurt, all beef broth, the flour and the egg. Use a hand blender to blend well. Turn heat on medium and start stirring the sauce constantly until it comes to a boil. This takes nearly fifteen minutes, without changing direction of the stirring, otherwise, the yogurt will start separating. When the mixture comes to a boil start adding one meatball at a time while stirring gently. When all meatballs have risen to the top they are cooked. Add 1 can of garbanzo beans without juice, the dried mint, dried dill, the chopped parsley, and the cooked rice and stir. Let it cook for another 5-8 minutes. Add salt to taste. Allow the soup to cool 10 minutes before serving.

Serve with lawasha or Samoon on a cold day.

**Assyrian Dikhwa**

1 pound beef with bones or 1 pound shoulder lamb with bones
4 cups plain yogurt
1 egg beaten
1 cup pearled barley
1 teaspoon salt
30 cups Water

In a large pot combine the meat with 10 cups water, teaspoon salt and bring to boil. Reduce heat and simmer on low for 1 hour. When the meat is tender, strain the liquid if any left.

While the meat is cooking, use a separate pot to combine the barley, 1/2 teaspoon salt and 10 cups water. Bring to boil. Cover and simmer for 40 minutes. Strain the liquid and rinse the barley and strain again.

In a new pot mix the yogurt and the egg, and beat well. Add 10 cups water, and 1/2 teaspoon salt and stir. Bring the yogurt mixture to a boil, stirring without stop and reduce heat. Add the meat, the barley and cook on low for about an hour without covering.

Serve with lawasha or Samoon and enjoy

**Assyrian Gurdu**

1/4 cup short grain rice soaked for 1/2 hour
3 cups hot water
3 cups cold water
3 1/2 cups plain yogurt
1 teaspoon salt

In a large pot over medium heat combine the hot water with rice and cook until the rice is soft and tender. Add 3 cups cold water and the yogurt and stir constantly. Add salt and stir constantly stirring until the soup is thickened.

Serve in a bowl and add butter to your taste.


**Assyrian Treeda-Assyrian cold Yogurt soup with bread**

1 cup yogurt
1/4 cup water
1 tablespoon chopped dill
1 cucumber chopped
Salt to taste
1 piece of bread broken

Mix the yogurt and water and beat well to combine. Add the rest of the ingredients to it and stir. Salt to taste. When ready to eat add the broken bread and mix. Enjoy on a hot summer day.


**Daweh-Doogh (yogurt drink)**

2/3 cup water
3-4 tablespoons yogurt
Pinch of salt
Optional-Pinch of dry mint.
In a glass combine and stir well. Add ice and enjoy a refreshing drink

## Assyrian Gupta-Cheese

1/2 gallon whole milk
1/4 cup lemon juice or white vinegar
1/4 teaspoon salt
Cheese cloth
Colander to strain the whey

In a large saucepan add 1/2 gallon whole milk. Heat on medium high stirring occasionally so the milk doesn't scald or burn. When the milk begins to rise and foam remove from heat and add 1/4 cup lemon juice or vinegar. This will cause the milk to curdle (seperate). Let the milk stand for 10 minutes.

Put a cheese cloth over the colander and pour the separated milk into the strainer. The liquid will drain and you'll have only the curds left. I Never discard the liquid but use it to make bread.

Gather the cloth and squeeze the rest of the liquid out of it. Sprinkle with salt and mix gently. Place the cheese with the cheese cloth on a plate. Shape into a square or a rectangle. Fold the cheese cloth over it, to cover it. Place a heavy pan on the cheese and let it shape the cheese for an hour. Remove the cheese cloth and wrap the cheese in plastic or place it in a Tupperware container with lid. You can use the cheese immediately or refrigerate until needed. Enjoy with olives and bread.


## Gupta Tumirta-Burried Cheese
We no longer have to bury the cheese. We can now use Kasseri cheese to make it.

1 pound Kasseri cheese
1/2 cup cumin seeds (mayana)

In a bowl crumble the Kasseri cheese or grind in a food processor. Add the cumin seeds and mix well. Store in a plastic container with a lid and refrigerate for at least 3 days. The cumin seeds will soften and infuse the cheese with flavor of cumin.

Serve with bread and chai. Assyrians use Gupta tumerta in a lawasha sandwich and enjoy it with chai.

# ASSYRIAN SALADS

## Assyrian Chopped Salad (zaladda)

4 cucumbers peeled and chopped
4 firm tomatoes chopped
1 minced onion
1/2 bunch cilantro de-stemmed, washed and chopped
Optional-1 chopped jalapeno (if you like heat)
salt to taste
4 tablespoons lemon juice
4 tablespoons olive oil

Chop all vegetables and place into a bowl. Add chopped cilantro and mix well. Add salt, lemon and virgin olive oil just before serving.

## Taboula

1/2 cup fine bulgur # 1 soaked in 1/2 cup of lemon juice for 20 minutes
3 bunches flat leaf parsley, de-stemmed, washed and finely chopped
3 bunches of green onions, washed and finely chopped
6 firm tomatoes finely chopped
1/2 cup extra virgin olive oil

In a large bowl mix all chopped vegetables and herbs. Add the soaked bulgur without squeezing the lemon juice out. Mix well. Add the olive oil and mix well.

Salt to taste before serving.

Serve with washed Romain lettuce. Assyrians like to take a piece of lettuce and fill it with Taboula and eat it that way. Try it in all ways.

## Assyrian Potato Salad

6 boiled potatoes that are still slightly firm, not mushy
10 cloves crushed garlic
3 bunches flat leaf parsley de-stemmed, washed and chopped
1 cup extra virgin olive oil
1/2 cup fresh lemon juice
Salt to taste

Peel cooled potatoes and cut them bite size. Place in a big bowl. Chop the parsley and add to bowl. Add all the crushed garlic and mix well. Add the lemon juice, the olive oil and salt to taste and mix to combine. Chill for one hour before serving.

## Assyrian Tomato salad

6 firm tomatoes washed and chopped
1 minced onion
1 tablespoon chopped flat leaf parsley
Salt and pepper to taste
1/4 cup olive oil
2 tablespoons lemon juice

Chop the tomatoes and onions well. Combine them in a bowl. Add the chopped parsley and salt and mix well again. Add lemon and oil mix well again. Let stand for 30 minutes before serving.


## Assyrian Chickpea Salad-Zaladda d'Khardamaneh

1 can Garbanzo beans strained
1 cup kalamata pitted olives sliced in half
3 unpeeled cucumbers chopped
2 tomatoes chopped
1 teaspoon salt
the juice of 1 lemon
1 bunch Romain lettuce washed and torn bite size
1/4 cup extra virgin olive oil
2 cloves crushed garlic
1 teaspoon dried mint
1 teaspoon tamarind sauce

In a jar combine the lemon juice, the oil, the garlic, the tamarind and the mint and mix well. Allow to rest 15 minutes to marinade.

Chop all vegetables and combine in a bowl. Add strained chickpeas and sliced olives and mix well with a spoon. Add the salt and the marinade and toss the salad.

Serve in a bowl and enjoy as a main meal with bread and soup or serve as a salad.

## Masta Khyar-Assyrian Yogurt Cucumber and Dill Salad

2 cups plain yogurt whipped with a fork
2 peeled and chopped cucumbers
1/2 bunch fresh dill de-stemmed, washed and chopped
1/4 teaspoon salt

In a bowl add the yogurt and beat with a fork until smooth. Add chopped cucumbers and dill and mix well. Add 1/4 teaspoon salt and mix well. Refrigerate and serve chilled.

## Assyrian Carrot and Raisin Salad

4 cups shredded carrots
1 cup raisins of your choice washed and soaked in water for 15 minutes
1/2 cup yogurt
1/2 teaspoon sugar
1 tablespoon tamarind sauce or lemon juice
1/4 cup chopped cilantro

In a small bowl combine the yogurt, tamarind and sugar. Stir and set aside for 10 minutes. In a large bowl combine shredded carrots, strained raisins, and toss. Add the marinated yogurt and stir well to combine. Cover and chill 1 hour before serving.

## Assyrian Chaqraqa (Dandelion) and Poorpookheena (Purslane) Salad

1 bunch Purslane chopped
2 bunches Dandelions chopped
1/2 bunch parsley chopped
2 tomatoes chopped
1/4 cup extra virgin olive oil
1/4 cup fresh lemon juice
2 large cloves crushed garlic
1/4 teaspoon salt
1/8 teaspoon black pepper
1/4 cup pomegranate seeds

In a jar combine the oil, lemon juice, garlic, salt and pepper. Shake well and let rest for 20 minutes to marinade.

De-stem the dandelions, the parsley and purslane, wash, pat dry and chop. In a bowl combine all the chopped herbs, the tomatoes and the pomegranate seeds and mix well.

Pour the dressing over the salad and toss. Let rest for 5 minutes before serving.

**My Everyday Tossed Salad**

1 Romain lettuce torn bite size
2 large cucumbers peeled and sliced bite size
2 large firm tomatoes sliced bite size or sliced cherry tomatoes
1/2 red onion thinly sliced
1/2 cup Garbanzo beans strained
1/2 cup extra virgin olive oil
1/2 cup fresh lemon juice
2 cloves crushed garlic
1/2 teaspoon sugar
1 teaspoon paprika
1 teaspoon dried mint

In a large bowl with lid combine all fresh vegetables. Mix well, cover and refrigerate.

My Salad Dressing
In a jar, combine the olive oil, lemon, crushed garlic, salt, sugar, paprika, and shake to combine. Add mint and shake well. Allow to marinade until you're ready to serve the salad.

Pour the marinade over the salad and toss well.

# ASSYRIAN PASTAS

## Assyrian Spagetti

1 pound lean ground beef
1 minced onion
4 cloves crushed garlic
2 tablespoons curry powder
1 8-oz can tomato sauce mixed with 1 tablespoon tomato paste
1/2 of a 24 ounce package of spaghetti or 340 milligrams OR 1 7-oz
package of elbow macaroni
1/3 cup oil
1 teaspoon salt
1/2 teaspoon black pepper
1 cup water
Water and 1 tablespoon salt for boiling the spaghetti

In large pot filled halfway with water, 1 tablespoon salt, bring to boil. Add cut up
spaghetti or half package of elbow macaroni and cook 5 minutes only. It should be al
dente.

In a separate pot, add 1/3 cup oil and heat. Add the ground beef and break down till
browned but juicy. Add 1 minced onion and crushed garlic and sauté 3-5 minutes. Add 2
tablespoons curry powder and sauté 1 minute. Add tomato sauce/tomato paste mixture
and sauté 2 minutes. Add 1 cup water, the salt, the pepper and stir well. Turn heat down
to low and cover pot. Allow meat to simmer until spaghetti is cooked and strained
through a colander. Combine the two pots and mix well. Cover and simmer on very low
for 5-10 minutes. Allow to cool 5 minutes before serving.

Serve with a nice salad of your choice and some Assyrian garlic bread
sticks.

## Assyrian Vegetarian Macaroni for Soma

1 7-oz package elbow macaroni
1 sliced carrot
1 chopped Zuchini
1 8-oz can tomato sauce mixed with 2 tablespoons tomato paste
1/2 bunch de-stemmed, washed and chopped parsley
1 minced onion
3 cloves crushed garlic
1 tablespoon curry powder
1 tablespoon paprika
1 teaspoon turmeric
1/2 cup water
2 teaspoons salt separated
1/2 teaspoon black pepper
1/3 cup oil

In a large saucepan add 1/3 cup oil and heat on high. Add 1 minced onion and sauté 2-3 minutes. Add the paprika, the turmeric and sauté 1 minute. Add the tomato sauce/paste combo and sauté 2 minutes. Add the carrots and sauté 2-3 minutes. Add the zucchini and sauté 2-3 minutes. Add the garlic, the parsley, 1/2 cup of water, 1 teaspoon salt and 1/2 teaspoon pepper and stir.

In a large pot half filled with water, add 1 teaspoon salt and bring to boil. Add the macaroni and cook for 5 minutes only. Strain in a colander. Add the cooked and strained macaroni to the sautéed vegetables pan. Stir to combine. Turn heat to low and simmer 5 minutes.

Serve with salad and some Samoon.

If you don't like zucchini you can substitute with peas instead, or any vegetable you like.

**My son Sam's Fettucini**, which he calls FettaTrini, for our house keeper, Trinidad, "Trini."

1/2 package Fettucini noodles
1 cup cream
1/2 cup whole milk
1 tablespoon butter
1/2 cup peas
3 cloves crushed garlic
1/4 cup parmesan cheese
2 teaspoons salt

In a large pot filled half way with water, add 1 teaspoon salt and bring water to boil. Add the noodles and cook 5 minutes only.

In another pot or deep pan melt the butter. Add garlic and sauté 1 minute. Add 1/2 cup thawed peas and sauté 2-3 minutes. Add the cream, the milk, 1/4 cup parmesan cheese and sauté another minute. Add 1 teaspoon salt and stir well.

When noodles are cooked al dente, strain and combine with the sauce and stir well. Cover the pot and let it rest for a few minutes before serving.


**Sam's Linguini**

1/2 package linguini noodles
1 bunch parsley de-stemmed, washed and chopped
5 cloves crushed garlic
2 tablespoons butter
2 tablespoons oil
1/2 cup white wine
the juice of 1 lemon
1 teaspoon salt
2 tablespoons capers
Water and 1 tablespoon salt for boiling the noodles

In a large pot half filled with water and 1 tablespoon salt, bring to boil. Add linguini noodles and cook 5 minutes only.

In a large pan melt butter and add garlic and sauté 1 minute. Add oil, lemon and wine and stir well. Add 1 teaspoon salt and stir well. Allow the sauce to cook 2-3 minutes for the alcohol to evaporate.

When noodles are cooked, combine with the sauce and add the parsley.
Stir well and let rest 2 minutes. Serve with a salad and some garlic bread sticks

# THE BAKERY-Assyrian Desserts

Kullecha is an Assyrian compound word and comes from the Akkadian word Kuku, meaning cake, and lesha, which means dough. Today it is pronounced KULECHA Instead of KULESHA, meaning sweetened bread/dough. The same goes for the word Lawasha, which also comes from the word lesha and simply means to open the dough.

Ancient Assyrian tablets attest to the fact that any sweet breads such as cakes, cookies sweet breads were called Kuku, meaning cake. The Arabic word Ka'ak comes from the word Kuku which is further testament to their origin.

It is also well documented that the Assyrians were the first to make Baqlawa. This is also a compound Assyrian word that combines Baqla which means diamond shape and lawasha, which is very thin Assyrian dough, and has over the years turned into Baqlawa. The Iraqis inherited everything Assyrian/Mesopotamian civilization invented, and through time these became national Mesopotamian, or today's Iraq's national foods.

Today, most Middle Eastern people make these Assyrian delicacies, which were spread across Asia Minor through trade. When the Greeks colonized Assyria, they also took the Baqlawa recipe home with them.

The recipes in this book are mostly my mother's recipes. She was famous for her delicious food and baked goods. The recipe for Nazook was my grandmother's Anna Yonan, whom I was named after.


Here's an excerpt from Leaf.tv

"The Assyrians are credited with taking the first step toward the development of what we now relish as baklava. It was a rough pastry filled with nuts and honey. This empire controlled the ancient Near East in the eighth century BC."

## BAQLAWA

You will need:
1 package Fillo dough
2 sticks butter melted
Baqlawa filling
Simple Syrup
cookie sheet
2 cups coarsely ground walnuts
2 tablespoons lemon juice
Cardamom
Chopped pistachios for garnish
A good brush

The filling:
2 cups coarsely ground walnuts
1 1/2 tablespoons hail (ground cardamom)
1/4 cup sugar
2 tablespoons water

In a bowl combine 2 cups roughly ground walnuts with the cardamom, and the sugar. Mix well. Add 2 tablespoons water to the mixture to make it stick together. This will hold the filling in place.

Simple Syrup:
4 cups sugar
2 cups water
2 tablespoons lemon juice
1/2 cup honey

In a saucepan combine the sugar, the honey and the water and mix well until all sugar is dissolved. On high heat bring to boil 10-15 minutes or until syrup begins to get a bit thicker. Add 2 tablespoons lemon juice and continue to cook another 5 minutes. Remove from heat and set aside.

Making the Baqlawa

Butter the cookie sheet with a brush. Open the package of Fillo dough and unroll it on a towel and lay it flat. Place another towel over the stacks of Fillo dough so they don't dry out. Take one sheet of Fillo dough at a time and place in the greased cookie sheet. Brush it with butter, making sure all the sides and corners are buttered as well. Repeat with each sheet until half of the stack of Fillo sheets are buttered and layered in the pan. Pour the filling all over the buttered and stacked sheets of Fillo. Take another sheet of Fillo and place it over the walnut filling. Butter the sheet well. Repeat until the second stack of Fillo sheets are all buttered and stacked over the walnut mixture. Cut the baqlawa with a sharp knife into diamond shapes.

Bake at 350 degrees until golden brown (about 20 minutes) depending on whether the oven is electric or gas. Just make sure you keep watching it and remove it when it is golden brown. Remove the baked Baqlawa from the oven and immediately drizzle syrup over it. You may not need all the syrup you made. Sprinkle with chopped pistachios.

For cream filled Baqlawa-Make the above Baqlawa recipe without a filling and cut into squares, instead of diamond shape. Take each baked and syrupy Baqlawa square and separate one half from the other. Fill the bottom half with Gemar (breakfast cream) and place the top half over it. Press gently and place on a tray. Repeat with each square. Sprinkle with chopped pistachios.

**Assyrian Date And Walnut Bars**

Preheat oven at 350 degrees Fahrenheit

1 1/2 cups blanched almond flour
1/4 teaspoon sea salt
1/4 teaspoon baking powder
3 large eggs
1/4 cup oil
1/4 cup honey
1 tablespoon vanilla
1 cup walnuts
1 cup pitted and chopped dates

In a large bowl, combine almond flour and baking soda and mix well.

In another bowl combine eggs, oil, honey and vanilla, and mix well.

Combine both bowls and mix well. Fold in the dates and walnuts and mix well.

Pour the batter into a greased 8x8 inch baking dish. Bake for 20-30 minutes or until the top is golden brown. Insert a tooth pick to see if it is completely baked.

Allow to cool before cutting into squares.

**Dates stuffed with Walnuts**

30 dates Diqlat Noor or Medjool
30 walnut halves

Gently slit each date and remove the pit. Insert half a walnut inside the date and close the date. Set on a tray. Repeat with each date.

## ASSYRIAN KULECHA

5 pounds flour
1 can carnation evaporated milk
6 eggs whipped
2 1/2 lbs melted butter ((5 cups)
1 packet or 1 tablespoon dry yeast
1/2 cup sugar mixed into the flour
1/2 teaspoon salt to mix with dry yeast
1/2 teaspoon sugar to mix with dry yeast

In a small bowl, mix 1/2 teaspoon salt, 1/2 teaspoon sugar with 1 tablespoon dry yeast. Add a few tablespoons boiled but lukewarm water over the yeast. Stir well and set aside for at least 1/2 hour.

Mix 5 pounds of flour with 1/2 cup of sugar. Mix well to combine. Add the melted butter to the flour and begin mixing. Add the yeast to the flour and mix well. Add the evaporated milk and mix well. Whip the eggs and add them to the dough mixture. Knead the dough with your hands until it forms a smooth and cohesive dough. Cover the bowl with plastic then a thick blanket and let rise for at least 1 hour. Then knead again and let rise again for another 20 minutes, covered with plastic and blanket.

While the dough is rising prepare the filling.

Date Filling:
2 packages of pitted dates or 2 pounds of pitted and chopped dates.
1/4 cup ground cardamom (hail)
4 tablespoons oil

In a microwave, heat the dates for 1-2 minutes. Add the oil and mix well to combine. Add the hail and mix well again. If you don't like to use the microwave, then heat the dates stove top- In a saucepan heat the oil on medium and add the dates. Keep stirring to combine and not allow the dates to scorch. You may want to use a double boiler (dates in a pan over a pan full of boiling water), to heat the dates. Add the hail and stir well to combine.

Walnut filling:
1 pound ground walnuts (2 1/4 cups)
1/4 cup ground cardamom (hail)
1/2 cup sugar.
1/8 cup melted butter

Mix all ingredients to combine

Date Kuleche

Cut the dough in half, (half for walnut kuleche and the other half for date kuleche).

Divide one of the halves into equal parts for the date kuleche. Take each small mound of dough and open it with a rolling pin, making the dough as thin as possible, (1/8 of an inch thickness). Do the same with date mixture, making it into same size as the open dough. The easiest way to do this is to sprinkle some water on the counter and put a large sheet of plastic wrap over it. This makes the plastic stick to the counter and not move. Place the same amount of dates on the plastic wrap as the mound of dough you just opened. Open it with your hands first, spreading the dates as far as you can. Now place a plastic piece over the dates and roll it out with a rolling pin. The rolled date sheet should be nearly the size of the opened dough sheet. Transfer the rolled out date sheet and place it on the opened dough, making sure the dough circle is completely covered with date mixture. Take the edge of the dough from one end and roll it across all the way to the other end of the dough, as if you're rolling a carpet. Once the entire thing is rolled it will look like a log. Press the top gently with a rolling pin to flatten it out a bit. Cut the log into 1 inch slices. Place each one on a cookie sheet. Brush them with egg wash.

Egg Wash-Beat together 4 eggs with 1 teaspoon yogurt, making sure it is well blended.

Walnut Kuleche

Take the other half of the dough that you reserved for walnut kuleche and divide into small, equal mounds. With a rolling pin open each mound as thin as possible. With the mouth of a glass, cut small circles of dough. Spoon the walnut mixture on one side of the dough circle. Fold the other side of the dough over the filling. Brush the circle inside edges with some of the egg wash and press the edges together to seal them. Now crimp the edges as shown in the picture below. Place each finished kuleche on a cookie sheet. Brush with egg wash.

Bake the kuleche in a preheated oven at 350 degrees Fahrenheit for 20 minutes or until golden brown.

You can freeze what you don't consume, storing in plastic and then in a tupperware. When you have company, take them out of the freezer 1 hour before serving them. Or if you're in a hurry, warm them up in a microwave for a few seconds.

Mine never last long enough to freeze them. Every member of my family wants their share.

## Assyrian Nazookeh

3 cups flour
1/4 cup powdered sugar
1 cup plain yogurt
2 tablespoons whole milk
1 cup butter (2 sticks) room temperature
1 package or 2 1/2 tablespoons dry yeast

Egg Wash-2 eggs beaten and mixed with 1 teaspoon yogurt.

In a small bowl, add the yeast to the yogurt and mix well. Set aside for 5 minutes. Sift flour into a large mixing bowl. Add the sugar and mix well. Add the butter and mix well. Add the yogurt and mix well. Add the milk and mix well. Knead until dough is smooth and consistent. Wrap in plastic and refrigerate 1 hour.

Filling
2 cups ground walnuts
1 cup flour
1/2 cup sugar
1 cup butter

Melt the butter in a saucepan, add the flour and brown slightly until golden. Remove from heat and add the walnuts and sugar and mix well. It will look like a crumble. Set aside to cool.

Divide the dough in 4 equal pieces.

Take a piece of dough and roll it out with a rolling pin, and form into a long sheet of thin dough. Spoon filling evenly all over the dough. Cut the dough in half. Bring in one of the edges of the dough and begin to roll it all the way to the other end of the dough, as if you're rolling a carpet. Flatten it out gently with a rolling pin. With a crimping knife cut into 1 inch pieces and place on a cookie sheet lined with parchment paper. Repeat until all nazookeh are made.

Brush with egg wash and bake for 20-25 minutes in a preheated oven at 300 degrees Fahrenheit, until golden.

Serve with Assyrian tea (Chai).

**Sweet Kadeh**

Preheat oven at 400 F.

The dough

6 eggs whipped
5 pounds or 18 cups flour
1 1/2 pounds or 7 cups (14 sticks) unsalted butter melted
1 large or 2 small cans of carnation evaporated milk
16 ounce half and half
3 tablespoons yeast

Melt the butter, then cool. Combine the half and half and carnation evaporated milk and mix well. In a separate bowl, beat the eggs. In a large bowl add the melted butter and the milk mixture and 1 cup flour at a time and have the mixer ready in hand while you add the beaten eggs. Now add 1 cup of flour at a time until all 5 pounds of flour are mixed with eggs. Now add the yeast and work the dough by hand, not mixer. Let the dough rise for at least 8 hours. You can make the dough at night and wake up to a risen dough. Now divide the dough into 12 equal parts. Sprinkle the mounds with a bit of flour and cover in plastic for another 20 minutes till ready to make kadeh.

Sweet filling (martookha khilya)

10 sticks unsalted and melted butter
12 cups flour
1 cup sugar
1/4 cup oil

In a large pan, melt the unsalted butter. Slowly add the flour and keep stirring. Add 1/4 cup oil and keep stirring. Add 1 cup sugar and keep stirring for a total of 30-50 minutes or until the flour is toasted to golden brown. Don't let it stick or burn. Set aside to cool.

You can also bake this mixture in the oven at 300 degrees Fahrenheit. Spread the mixture in a cookie sheet and bake for half an hour.

Sprinkle the work surface with flour. Take one mound of dough at a time and open it with a rolling pin. Each time you work a mound put flour under it before opening it with a rolling pin. Turn the dough over and put more flour underneath until you've opened the dough into a large circle 1/8 inch in thickness. Spoon some sweet filling and spread it on one side of the dough. Gather the other side of the dough and fold it over the filling. Brush the inside edges with the egg and yogurt mixture and press the edges together with your fingers. Now go over the pressed edges with a fork making indents all around to seal.

Once you have made the kadeh, put each one on a cookie sheet lined with parchment paper.

Mix 6 eggs and 2 tablespoons yogurt, making sure it's mixed well. Brush each kada with this egg and yogurt mixture. With a fork, press the teeth of the fork into the dough (top of the kada).

Bake in preheated oven at 400 degrees Fahrenheit until light brown. Remove from oven and allow to cool on a rack.

Cut cooled kada into squares and serve with chai

**Assyrian Halwah**

2 cups flour
1 cup Butter
1/2 cup Nepookhta (grape molasses)
1 teaspoon lemon juice

In a sauce pan melt the butter over medium heat. Add the flour and turn flame to high. Cook the flour until golden brown, constantly stirring. Remove from heat. Pour in the molasses and mix well. Place the halwa in a deep dish while it's hot. Decorate it as you like. Allow to set 2-3 hours. Slice as needed into squares or diamond shapes.

## Assyrian Fisteqeh and Takhin Halwa-Assyrian Pistachio and Tahini Halwah

1 cup sugar
1/2 cup water
2 cups Tahini
1/2 cup pistachios
1 teaspoon rose water
Pistachios for garnish

In a saucepan combine the water and sugar and bring to boil on high heat. Boil 5-10 minutes and remove from heat.

In a separate sauce pan heat the Tahini and stir well.

Combine the two pots and stir well. Add the pistachios and stir well. Set aside to cool .

In a loaf pan lined with parchment paper, place some pistachios on the bottom. Spoon all the halwa mixture into the loaf pan and press to mold it. Refrigerate overnight.

Slice into squares or diamond shapes.

Serve with Assyrian chai.


## Coconut, Walnut, Date Bites

1/2 cup walnuts
1/2 cup shredded coconuts
1/2 cup coconut flakes
14 Diqlat Noor dates or Medjool dates pitted and chopped
1 pinch salt

Add the walnuts, dates, Shredded coconut, and salt to a food processor and process into a paste. Transfer into a greased bowl. Roll the mixture into 8 balls and roll into the coconut flakes.

Store in a tightly sealed container in the fridge. It will last weeks.

**Mom's Walnut Raisin cake**

Preheat oven to 350 degrees Fahrenheit.

4 eggs room temperature
2 sticks butter softened.
1 cup whole milk
3 cups flour
2 teaspoons baking powder
1 1/2 cups sugar
1/4 cup orange zest
1 cup crushed walnuts
1/2 cup raisins
1 tablespoon vanilla

Sift the flour and the baking powder into a bowl. In a mixing bowl combine the butter and sugar and mix well until sugar is dissolved. Add the eggs one a time and mix well. Add the Vanilla and mix well. Add the flour and milk gradually and mix well. Fold in the walnuts and raisins, the orange zest and mix well.

Grease the cake pan and sprinkle with flour. Pour the batter into the cake pan and spread evenly. Bake in the oven for 1 hour or until tooth pick comes out clean.

Remove the cake and allow to cool for one hour. With a knife release the edges. Put a plate on the pan and turn the pan upside down.

Serve with chai.

**Rabee Youab I. Yonan's signature cake**

This is our family's favorite cake because dad used to make it for us whenever we flew in or drove from out of town to visit our parents. It has become known as Papa's Cake because all his kids, grandkids and great grandkids love it the best. The house would be filled with the smell of this cake dad baked for us when he knew we were coming to visit. it reminds us of all the good times we had together whenever we were all together celebrating birthdays, graduations, Christmas or Easter.

**Papa's Cake**

My father, Rabee Youab I Yonan didn't waste time measuring and spooning. He was a writer and a scholar but he loved making us a cake whenever we'd visit. He'd buy a box of yellow cake and make it his own. Here's his recipe immortalized. It's great for last minute company too. Very impressive. With my busy life, being my elderly mother's sole caretaker for the last few years, this is what I use the most now, Papa's cake.

Preheat oven at 350 degrees Fahrenheit

1 box/package yellow cake mix
1 cup orange juice
1 cup crushed walnuts
1/4 cup freshly grated orange zest

Follow the package instructions by adding 3 eggs and oil or butter, but substitute the cup of water with freshly squeezed orange juice. Beat 3-4 minutes. Add 1/4 cup orange zest and 1 cup crushed walnuts. Mix well.

Grease the cake pan, and sprinkle flour all over it. Pour the batter into the cake pan and spread evenly. Bake in the oven for 1 hour. Test with a toothpick. If it comes out clean it is done. Remove the cake and allow to cool for one hour. With a knife release the edges. Put a plate on the pan and turn the pan upside down so the cake can lay on the plate.

No one in my family likes frosting so I don't frost it. But you can. I frost it for special occasions and decorate it with pineapple. You can decorate any which way you want.

Serve with chai.

OPTIONAL-Cream Cheese frosting

1/2 cup butter
4 cups powdered sugar sifted
1 8-ounce cream cheese package
1 teaspoon vanilla extract

In a mixing bowl combine butter and cream cheese and mix well. Gradually add sifted powdered sugar and mix well .

## Assyrian Date and walnut cake

Preheat oven to 350 degrees Fahrenheit.

1 cup pitted and chopped dates
1 egg beaten
1 cup milk
1/2 cup butter
1 cup sugar
1 teaspoon baking soda
1 1/2 cups flour
1 teaspoon vanilla
1 cup chopped walnuts

Grease a cake pan and sprinkle with flour.

In a saucepan over medium heat, combine the dates and milk and bring to boil. Add 1/2 cup butter and 1 cup sugar. Stir until butter is melted and sugar is dissolved. Remove from heat and let cool for 10 minutes. Add baking soda and stir. Let mixture rest for 10 minutes.

In a bowl combine date mixture with flour, eggs and vanilla and mix well. Add 1 cup chopped walnuts.

Pour batter into the greased and floured cake pan. Bake at 350 degrees Fahrenheit for 1 hour. Insert a tooth pick and if it comes out clean then it's done. If not, bake for another 5 minutes or so and try again.

Serve with chai and enjoy.

**Rice Pudding-**This pudding originates in the Persian region of Assyria, and it is called SholaZard in Parse. However, this is my own recipe

1 cup Jamine rice soaked 20 minutes
10 cups water
1 cup sugar

In a saucepan combine all three ingredients and mix well. On medium heat cook the rice in the sugar water stirring occasionally for 30 minutes. Reduce heat and simmer on low, covered to capture the steam and fluff the rice. When all the water is evaporated, test to see if the rice has been cooked down to a pudding consistency. If it hasn't, add more water and simmer longer, occasionally beating the rice with a wooden spoon to break it down, as if you're whipping it.

Flavoring the rice pudding

1 teaspoon ground saffron
1/4 cup hot water
1/4 cup Rose water

In a cup combine saffron threads with boiling water and set Aside. When the pudding is cooked, add 1/4 cup rose water to the pudding and mix well. Add the Saffron water and mix well. Cook for a few more minutes. Remove from heat and pour into a serving dish and decorate with Cinnamon powder and chopped pistachio nuts. Chill in the refrigerator before serving.

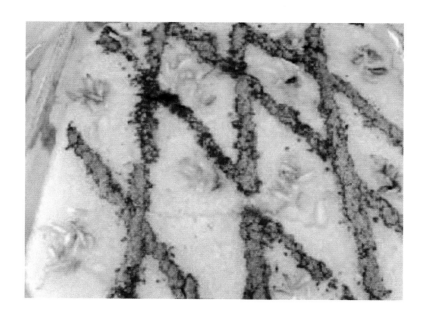

## Sheera dKhalwa-Assyrian Rice Pudding with milk

1 cup short grain rice (Calrose) or even Jasmine rice, soaked for 1 hour
2 cups whole milk
2 cups water
1/2 cup sugar
1/2 teaspoon salt
1 tablespoon rose water or orange blossom whichever you like
1/2 cup raisins
1/4 cup chopped pistachio nuts for garnish

In a sauce pan add 1 cup soaked rice and 2 cups water, 1/2 teaspoon salt. Mix well and bring to boil. Place a tin under the pan, cover the saucepan, turn heat to low and let the rice simmer until nearly all water is evaporated. Add the milk and sugar and stir well to combine. Add the raisins and stir again. On low heat, simmer for another 30 minutes. Add 1 tablespoon rose water and stir. Allow to rest for 20 minutes before serving. Pour mixture into a deep dish. Sprinkle with ground pistachio nuts.

This can be eaten warm on a cold day or cold on a hot day. When it is eaten hot it warms the entire body. When eaten cold it is very refreshing.

## Assyrian Namoura

The Syrup:
1/2 cup water
1 1/4 cups sugar
1 teaspoon lemon juice
1 tablespoon rose Water
1 tablespoon Orange Blossom Water

In a saucepan over medium heat, combine all ingredients. Stir to dissolve sugar and bring to boil for 8 minutes. Add 1 teaspoon rose water, 1 teaspoon orange blossom water. Bring to boil again. Add 1 tablespoon butter, and stir to dissolve over low heat. Remove the syrup and allow to cool.

Preheat oven at 350 degrees Fahrenheit
The Batter:
1 cup sifted flour
1 1/2 cup semolina (smeed)
1 cup sugar
12 blanched and peeled almonds
1 cup milk
1/2 cup oil
1 1/2 teaspoon baking powder

In a bowl, combine the flour, the semolina, the sugar, and the baking powder. Mix well.

Gradually add the milk, the oil and whisk together. Pour into a greased baking dish. Slice the Namoura any which way you want, whether squares or diamond shape cuts. Decorate with blanched and peeled whole almonds. Bake at 350 degrees Fahrenheit for 40 minutes until golden brown. Pour the syrup all over immediately. After an hour retrace the cuts and cut the cake into squares or diamonds. Serve with your favorite beverage

## Assyrian Namoura with Gemar/Qishda

Pour half of the Namoura dough on the cookie sheet and spread evenly. Add a layer of Gemar, (cream), and spread evenly over the dough. Now add the second half of the dough and layer over the cream and spread it evenly. Bake at 350 degrees Fahrenheit for 40 minutes or until golden brown. Drizzle all of the syrup over it immediately. Allow to cool for 3-4 hours before cutting into shapes. Grind 1/2 cup of pistachios and sprinkle all over it.

## Zulabia

2 3/4 cup warm water
2 1/2 cups flour
1/2 teaspoon sugar
1 1/2 tablespoons or 1 envelop yeast
1/2 cup cornstarch
1/2 teaspoon salt
1 tablespoon orange blossom
Oil for frying
Simple sugar
1/4 cup chopped pistachios

In a bowl combine 1 cup of the warm water and the yeast. Let rest 5 minutes. Add the flour, sugar, salt, cornstarch, orange blossom and mix well. Let sit 20 minutes. Stir well again to dissolve all bubbles.

Heat oil on high. Place all the dough in a piping bag or pour into a plastic bottle with a narrow spout. Pipe or drizzle the dough in a circular motion into the hot oil. Cook until light golden brown on both sides, turning often. Place fried Zulabia on paper towel to drain.

Simple Syrup:

1 cup water

2 cups sugar
1 tablespoon lemon juice

In a saucepan, combine water and sugar, stir well to dissolve.  Bring to boil for 15 minutes. Add lemon juice and stir well. Remove from heat. Transfer to a bowl.

Dip cooked zulabia into the syrup and place on a dish. Sprinkle with ground pistachios.

## Znood Al Sit-Kahee with Qishda

1 package Spring roll wrap
1 cup whole milk
1 cup whipping cream
2 teaspoons rose water
1/4 cup ground pistachios
3 tablespoons corn starch
Simple Syrup

In a saucepan combine milk, cream and cornstarch and blend well. On medium heat keep stirring and bring to boil. Remove and add 2 teaspoons rose water. Let cool and form into a solid form.

Take each Spring roll sheet and fill with cooled cream, (qishda). Fold the edges and roll from one end to the other. Brush some milk on the edge to seal the roll.

Heat oil on high. Fry each roll on both sides until golden brown. Remove each fried roll and dip in syrup. Sprinkle with ground pistachios.

**Manna-Manna Al Samma**
2 cups sugar
1/4 teaspoon salt
1/4 cup water
2 egg whites
1 1/2 cups corn syrup
1 teaspoon cardamom
1/4 cup butter
1 1/2 cups toasted almonds, walnuts, pistachios, and pecans
Flour for storing the manna

In a saucepan combine sugar, corn syrup, salt and water and mix well. Over medium heat stir the mixture to dissolve sugar and form the syrup. Test the syrup by dropping a drop of it on the counter. It should become stiff, not runny. If it stiffens, it is done.

While the syrup is cooking, Beat 2 egg whites until firm and shiny. Add 1/4 cup syrup to the eggs and keep whipping. Cook the remainder syrup longer until it thickens. Test the syrup to see if it has cooked long enough by taking a spoonful and dropping it into a glass of water. If it forms into a ball then it's ready. Add the syrup to the egg mixture and keep whipping until it forms taffy like substance. Fold in the the butter, cardamom and the nuts.

Spread the taffy into a greased and then floured cookie sheet. Set aside for at least 12 hours or more. Cut into small squares and with each square form into a ball. Dip into the flour to keep them from sticking. Store in a cool area and enjoy. The shelf life for this is fairly long but try to consume fresh within a week or two.


**Assyrian Shakarlamma-Sugar Cookies**

2 sticks unsalted butter room temperature
1 cup powdered sugar
2 cups flour
1 teaspoon ground cardamom
30 blanched and peeled almonds

Preheat oven at 350 degrees Fahrenheit

In a small saucepan filled halfway with water, bring to boil. Blanch the almonds for 1 minute. With a slotted spoon remove almonds and place in a bowl of cold water. Peel the almonds and place on a kitchen towel to dry.

In a bowl, using a hand mixer beat the butter until fluffy. Add powdered sugar and beat until smoothly blended. Mix the flour and cardamom together. Gradually add the flour and cardamom mixture to the butter and beat until the flour is well combined.

Remove dough from mixer and with your hands form a ball, cover with plastic and refrigerate at least 1/2 hour. Remove the dough from refrigerator and take a small pinch in your hand and form a ball. Now roll the ball between your hands until it starts to elongate like a snake. Bring the ends together and crisscross. Place a blanched almond on the crisscross. Place the formed Shakarlemma on a well greased cookie sheet.

Repeat until all dough is made into the shape, or the shape of your choice. Bake in the oven for 15 minutes. Do not allow the cookies to brown. Cool the cookies before removing them from the cookie sheet.

## Date Halwa

2 pounds pitted and softened dates
1 pound chopped walnuts
1 tablespoon ground cardamom
1/2 cup toasted sesame seeds
4 tablespoons flour
1/2 stick butter

Grind the cardamom. Melt the butter in a saucepan and add the flour. Sauté until it starts to bubble and turn golden. Add the dates and break down while cooking in the saucepan, about 5-7 minutes. Remove from heat and add 1 tablespoon ground cardamom. Mix well and set aside to cool.

On a cookie sheet lined with parchment paper, spread some walnuts. Take half of the date paste and roll it out with a rolling pin between two parchment papers. It should be rolled out as big as the cookie sheet.

Transfer the rolled out date and place it on top of the walnuts. Place parchment paper over the dates and with a rolling pin spread the dates evenly. Remove the parchment paper. Place another layer of walnuts on top of the date sheet. Roll out the rest of the dates on the counter, between 2 pieces of parchment paper. Transfer it to the cookie sheet and place on top of the walnuts. Sprinkle toasted sesame seeds all over the date sheet. Press the layers with a rolling pin to smooth it out evenly.

Place in the refrigerator for at least an hour. On a cutting board turn the pan upside down. Remove the cookie sheet. Cut the date layers into squares.

## FRUITS AND NUTS

Fruits and nuts are very important part of everyday Assyrian life, not just holidays. You'll never walk into an Assyrian household without finding some assorted fruits and nuts on the coffee table or the dining room table.

Most Assyrians owned their own vineyards and orchards no matter what region of Assyria they lived. They grew every kind of nut you could think of and every kind of fruit, besides grapes.

Assyrians are proud of their farming skills, pruning and tending their vineyards and orchards constantly. Many Assyrians migrated to the US around the turn of the century, opening various businesses on the Eastern shores of the United States, such as New York, New Jersey, Boston, even Connecticut, but soon they began to leave the east coast and the Midwest for Turlock simply because they had missed their orchards and vineyards.

In Assyria, most of the grapes would be ready by August and marked the event on (Shara D'Mart Maryam) St. Mary's Festival, August 15th. That's how everyone knew the grapes are ripe to pick for their tables, to make their wines and to hang clusters of grapes (tlooweh) from beams in their homes or their umber (storage rooms), and even their pagas, (barns). It was also a time to make raisins (kishmeesheh), to eat with their walnuts (Gozeh).

You might ask why St. Mary would be associated with the harvesting of grapes. This goes back to the days when Assyrians would give thanks to their goddess of love and fertility, Ishtar-Inanna, for the fertility and fruitfulness of her blessings which she bestowed upon them. There are many references of this in the Bible. Especially Jeremia, in which the women would say, "We will not listen to, (false prophets) we will worship the queen of heaven and pour drink libation unto her. For when we worshipped her we did not experienced anything unpleasant. But since we stopped worshipping her and pouring drink libations unto her we have been inflicted with famine and sword." Wise words to live by. When queen Shamiram died she was deified as the queen of heaven Ishtar and in the advent of Christianity Shamiram became Mariam (This is where the word Mariam comes from). Since the Assyrians were the first to become Christianized by Constantine, hence the association.

The grape festival would usher in the shaking of almonds, walnuts and pistachios. In the fall, every Assyrian household would store walnuts, almonds, pistachios, figs, raisins and other dried fruits, which were stored in their umbers and eaten all winter long. Even today that's what you'll find on our tables, no matter what time of the year it is.

Most Assyrians shell the walnuts themselves and they put walnut halves right next to the raisins, so that you can grab and mix them up and enjoy the combination of the two. There's nothing like it in the world. The other extraordinary flavor you can produce for a healthy snack is to stuff dates with walnuts. These two flavors are the favorite Assyrian snacks and they are healthy and rich in vitamins that you get from a good soil. There were a variety of grapes that the Assyrians cultivated for wine-making and most households made their own wines and Arak. They also made the best date and grape molasses. My grandmother Anna Yonan made Arak, wine, grape molasses and date molasses for Halwa. The grape molasses needs a special white ash found only in the Urmia region, and the hilly tops of Assyria.

Dates are a very important part of Assyrian life as the country is well known for some of the finest dates in the world. They are eaten as a snack, as a dessert, made into molasses, syrup, even alcoholic and nonalcoholic beverages as well as used in Assyrian cooking.

Pomegranates are an important fruit to the Assyrians. They're harvested in October and stored in cool storage (Umber) to be eaten all winter and we also make pomegranate juice and molasses with it.

**Assyrian Holidays**

Christmas is known as EID D'MOLADA or Eida Soora- The birth of the little one, whether it was Tammuz, Ninos, and later Jesus, (the sun/son).

Assyrian Christmas did not start with shopping and decorating. Our Christmas and Easter began with Soma (fasting). We fast 50 days before Christmas and 40 days of Lent before Easter. These traditions began with the Assyrian Queen Shamiram who compelled us to fast for 50 days and pray before the Messiah (her son Ninos) was born, and 40 days of Lent before her son was resurrected. These Assyrian traditions continued when we became the first nation to be Christianized. During Soma we prepare by cleansing our bodies, minds and souls, as well as our homes. We don't shop like crazy. We wash carpets, drapes, walls, and beddings to prepare for these holidays. We bake Kolecheh, kadeh, and we fatten turkeys and pigs for roasting.

Then on the eve of Christmas, and while children slept, the parents brought in an evergreen into the house and decorated it with candles and silver and gold just as the Bible says they did thousands of years ago. Jeremiah again, "They (the Assyrians) cut a tree from the forest with an axe, and they fasten it with nails so that it may not move. They deck it with silver and gold."

For more on the Origins of Christmas and Easter refer to my online articles.

https://www.facebook.com/Speakassyriaorg/posts/1081033465344870?__tn__=K-R

https://www.facebook.com/Speakassyriaorg/posts/2474312289350307?__tn__=K-R

My mother and her sister, aunt Joanne, would bake for weeks before Christmas. My dad would fatten the turkey on the roof for a whole month. Mom would stuff it the night before Christmas, while dad fastened the tree with a nail. While we slept my parents would decorate the tree. Christmas morning, we would wake up and the tree would be lit up like MAGIC.

Easter in Assyria was a time of renewal of nature and humanity. It was originally the Festival of Ishtar pronounced Easter (refer to my online article Assyrian Origins of Easter). It is known as Eida d'Qyamta, Festival of Resurrection of nature and therefore celebrated as the festival of fertility, which is why Easter is associated with eggs and bunnies.

Assyrians renewed themselves this time of the year and wearing new clothes and shoes symbolized that resurrection/renewal. In ancient Assyria died eggs that symbolized fertility of nature, through the Goddess of fertility, Ishtar who bore them all, were hung from temple walls. The Egg of the Euphrates as it turns out when washed ashore, out came Ishtar, the goddess of Love.

**SOMA GULLEH-Palgit Palloo or palgit Soma**

For fasting, the Assyrians make Gulleh, which is a vegetarian kadda half way through the 50 days of fasting before Christmas and halfway through fasting for 40 days of Lent before Easter. They make a cross out of grape vine, which is flexible wood and bake it inside the Gulleh. Whoever got the cross was blessed that year. According to my aunt Aglanteen, my dad would always get that cross in his Gulleh.


**Vegetarian Gulleh Recipe**

The Dough

3 1/2 cups flour
1 tablespoon dry yeast
1 cup warm water
1 teaspoon sugar
1/4 cup oil
1/2 teaspoon salt

In a large bowl add the yeast, sugar and 1/2 cup of warm water and mix well. Let stand until yeast is developed for 16 minutes. Add 1 cup flour and mix well. Gradually start adding the rest of the flour, salt until combined into a dough. Add the oil and work with your hands to knead the dough and form a smooth consistency. Cover and set aside in a warm place to rise for at least 2 hours.


The Filling

1 minced onion
2 cloves crushed garlic
1/2 can garbanzo beans, strained
1/2 can Red kidney beans strained
1 cup walnuts
1/2 teaspoon salt
1/2 teaspoon black pepper
1 tablespoon ground coriander seeds
1 teaspoon ground cumin seeds
1 tablespoon paprika
2 tablespoons oil

In a saucepan, add the oil and heat on high. Add the minced onion and garlic and sauté 2-3 minutes. Add the ground coriander, cumin and paprika and sauté 1 minute. Remove from heat.

In the food processor, add the walnuts and grind. Add the strained chickpeas and strained kidney beans and grind. Add the salt and pepper and mix well. Combine the bean mixture with the sautéed onions and mix well to combine. Set aside to cool.

Making the Gulleh Kada

Divide the dough into 4 equal parts. Open each dough ball with a rolling pin. Spoon the filling on 1 side of the open dough circle and spread it evenly on that side. Fold the other side of the dough over the filling. Wet the edges of the dough with water and seal the dough. Brush the top of the kadda with oil. With the teeth of a fork poke holes all over the Kada.

Bake in the oven at 400 degrees Fahrenheit for 20-25 minutes or until golden brown.

**Thanksgiving**

Assyrians of Diaspora celebrate Thanksgiving, living in their adopted countries. For Thanksgiving, I've learned to keep it simple since too much food spoils the appetite. I serve appetizers and drinks in the afternoon and dinner with white wine in the evening. Ecco Domani Pinot Grigio is a good pairing with Turkey.

**Turkey**-I thaw it out in the refrigerator for 2 days. The night before Thanksgiving I wash it, discard the giblets, pat dry, and salt it inside and out. I make a butter and spice rub mixture consisting of 1 softened butter, 1 teaspoon salt, 2 tablespoons red paprika, 1 teaspoon black pepper, and 1/4 cup garlic powder. Mix well to blend and rub all over the turkey, inside and out.

**The stuffing**-1 cookie sheet each of cut up and toasted white bread and wheat bread in the oven. In a saucepan, melt 1/2 stick butter. Add 1 chopped breast of chicken or turkey, 1 minced onion, 3 chopped stalks of celery, 1/2 bunch chopped parsley, and sauté 2-3 minutes, until chicken is cooked. Add 1 cup chicken broth and bring to boil. Combine the chicken and vegetable mixture with the toasted bread in a bowl and mix well. Add a pinch each of Rosemary, Sage, Thyme and mix well.

I stuff the turkey and leave it in the fridge overnight. I wake up early in the morning on Thanksgiving day and put the stuffed Turkey in the oven at 300 degrees Fahrenheit 5-6 hours with the pan covered, basting every hour with the Turkey juice. The last half hour, I uncover the lid and let the turkey get browned.

**Sweet potatoes**-Bake the sweet potatoes in the oven the night before. Allow to cool and peel. Slice the sweet potatoes and place in baking dish. In a saucepan melt 1/2 stick of butter, 1 teaspoon cinnamon powder, 1 cup walnuts. Sauté 3-4 minutes and add 1/4 cup brown sugar. Stir well to dissolve and pour the mixture all over the sweet potatoes. Thanksgiving day I bake it at 350 degrees Fahrenheit for 20-30 minutes.

**Green Bean Casserole**
2 bags of French cut Frozen green beans
1 minced onion
1 pint sour cream
1 cup crushed plain corn flakes
1 package of sliced Swiss cheese
1 stick of butter divided in half
1/2 teaspoon salt

Blanch the frozen green beans in boiling water and strain. In a large saucepan melt 1/2 stick of butter and add onions. Sauté 2-3 minutes. Add the strained green beans and sauté 2-3 minutes. Remove from heat and allow to cool for 3 minutes then mix in the sour cream, and 1/2 teaspoon salt to combine. Transfer green bean/sour cream mixture to a baking dish. Place sliced Swiss cheese over the beans, covering the entire dish.

Sprinkle with crushed corn flakes covering all the cheese. Melt the other 1/2 stick of butter and pour all over the corn flakes. Bake at 350 degrees Fahrenheit for 30 minutes until corn flakes are golden brown. Cut into squares.

**Mashed potatoes**-6 boiled and peeled potatoes. Place potatoes in a pot and over medium heat, add 1 cup milk, 1/2 stick of butter and 1 teaspoon salt. Mash well.

**Gravy**-In a saucepan, melt 1/2 stick butter. Add 1 minced onion and sauté. Add 2 tablespoons flour and sauté till golden brown. Add 4 cups turkey juice and stir well. Bring to boil. Taste to see if the gravy needs more salt. Gradually add salt. And stir.

I serve this dinner with my tossed salad, baked rice, baqleh Rice, bread Rolls, and cranberry sauce and tourshi. Pumpkin and apple pies and assortment of desserts with lots of chai or coffee to help us digest the Turkey and keep us awake.

Thanksgiving turkey should be tender and juicy on the inside and redish-brown on the outside.

## Assyrian Dookhrana-Religious Festivals Assyrians call SHARA

Assyrians have many religious festivals, all of which were centered around religious figures from the ancient times until they were finally Christianized. No other nation makes a dookhrana, (a sacrifice) to their ancient gods, goddesses and saints, all of whom are parts and parcels of Ashur, their one true god, and whose name sake they are, but the Assyrians. They continue to do so but disguised under Christian "saint days" just as Constantine wanted.

Making Dookhrana was a community event in Assyria. A particular family would make a sacrifice of a sheep, goat, Ram, depending on the region in which they lived in Assyria, to their favorite patron saint. Most of the time the neighborhood got together and donated to the cause by either contributing to the lamb cost or buying bread, gillaleh, tourshi and beverages for the cause.

They would pay the butcher who bought the lamb and brought it to them, along with his butchering skills. The butcher then slaughtered the lamb and cut it into pieces. Shoulders, shanks, ribs, feet, head, belly, arms, legs, even the brain. They would keep the brain, the head, the legs, the stomach (tripe) for Pacha (Reesh Aqleh). Every inch of the lamb was used, including the intestines, which were used to make basturmas. The edible meat would then be distributed to the poor in the name of their particular patron saint. The other way the community benefitted from dookhranas is that they began to cook it on either open fires, as in northern Assyria, or portable stoves brought to the courtyards and lit with kerosene or gas containers. They would place gigantic pots filled with lamb and water and cook it over these fires from sun-up till it was ready to be served. This would be an event that the entire community participated in, cooking and eating together and socializing.

You can tell them their Jesus was the final sacrifice all you want, but they'll say, "We know that, but it's a socializing, giving, sharing, and in service to god and other humans, together, the whole." Rich, poor, poverty-stricken, old, young, everyone in the neighborhood came together and had a feast by designating the tasks or sharing in the tasks. It is their devotion to the task that's important here. No job is too big, no lamb too costly, no bread shortage keeps them from fulfilling their duties and being devoted to the task. That's how they survived, despite the numerous genocides. As one Jewish scholar noted, "the Assyrian genocide went on for decades." Being devoted to the task then is a way of living and surviving for them.

That's why they are so devoted to the task of cooking. They spent so much time being devoted to the task of making tasty but healthy and nourishing food. In comparison, the so-called advanced Western world had centuries to use spices and flavors to develop exotic food but never got beyond the meat and potatoes phase. Being devoted to the task then is the key to success of anything, growing, cooking, eating nutritious, delicious food, which is why they were able to focus and build the greatest civilization on earth. No other nation ever did that, despite its own advantages and "advanced status", i.e. Super Powers. It is why our nation was called the Garden of Eden, where everything was possible. The sky was the limit. There was nothing they couldn't do.

In the Diaspora, Assyrians continue these religious traditions but inside their church yards or their cultural clubs, and on rare occasions in their individual backyards or garages.

The important thing is that this broth is very high in fat content, therefore, many hours are spent clearing the broth of all fat, (skimming the fat) which they call SAPETA, until a clear broth is achieved with tender pieces of meat. It is then served in bowls and the whole neighborhood partakes of this feast, especially the poor and the underprivileged, who were the original recipients of the dookhrana.

Before serving the dookhrana, tables would be set up filled with Gillaleh, (herbs) all sorts of breads, cheeses, tourshi and even garlic paste to add to each bowl if desired, and lots of jars of water and little salt bowls, for those who want to add more salt to the broth.

My mother had two girls, my sister Mary, then me. She wanted a boy very badly. Dad didn't care one way or another, as long as the babies were healthy. In fact, he wrote in his diary "I was happy I had another girl, Ann-Margret because girls bring families together, whereas boys get married and become sons to their in-laws." Truer words were never spoken!!!

Consequently my mother promised to make a sacrifice (dookhrana) if she had a boy. When my brother Edward was born, she sacrificed a lamb to him at the Ancient Church of the East in Baghdad, Mart Maryam, in Karrada d'Maryam district in Baghdad.

They brought the living lamb to the church yard and said to Eddie, "This is your lamb". Eddie was so happy to have a pet. Then the butcher took Eddie's foot and put it on the neck of the lamb, and off went his head. Eddie was traumatized. His pet had been slaughtered and sacrificed in an instant.

## ASSYRIAN BREAD

Bread was invented in Assyria due to the existence of plentiful and variety of grain available. In fact, that's why civilization began in Assyria, the Fertile Crescent, between two rivers, the Tigris and the Euphrates. From the Assyrian clay tablets, we know there were over 300 varieties of bread made in Assyria. Samoons, flat breads, lawasha, etc. But they also made sweet breads, cookies, cakes, etc., all of which were called Kuku in Akkadian, (ancient Assyrian language) from which the Arabic word Ka'ak comes.

From the time of Gilgamesh, Samoon was baked and this history is recorded on clay tablets. When Gilgamesh visits Utnapishtim to ask for the secret of ever lasting life, Utnapishtim's wife, Zamer Amit bakes a new loaf of bread for each day Gilgamesh sleeps. When he finally awakes he sees 12 loaves of bread, which is how many days he had slept. (Refer to my children's book, 'Gilgamesh, a Fairy Tale' for the story).

My father, Rabee Youab I Yonan was born in Camp Al Gailany, a district in Baghdad where the Assyrian refugees fleeing the Assyrian Genocide settled and built their homes of burnt mud-bricks. Although most households, including my father's, built a tanoor (a clay oven) inside their enclosed yards, where they baked Lawasha, Camp Al Gailany had a fantastic bakery near my father's childhood house. Everyday Samoon was baked at the bakery, put on carts and pulled through the streets of Gailany, yelling, "Samoon harr" (hot Samoon). This was my dad's favorite bread and as a child, he'd open a warm Samoon and fill it with Harissa. He would eat this for breakfast.

When I was writing this book, I did not intend to include a recipe for Samoon. But the night I finished typing the Harissa recipe for this book, my aunt Aglanteen had a dream in which my dad was making Harissa. In the dream he asks her to go get him a Samoon. When she brings it to him, he opens the Samoon and fills it with Harissa. The next morning my aunt tells me that she had a dream about her brother, my dad, making Harissa and asking her to bring him Samoon. This prompted me to include the Samoon recipe in this book, to honor my dad's message to me, "Harissa is no good without Samoon."

Rest in peace, dad. I have included the Samoon recipe in this book, in your honor and memory.

**Assyrian Samoon**

6 cups all purpose flour, sifted
1 envelope yeast, or 1 heaping tablespoon yeast
1/2 cup corn meal
2 teaspoons sugar
1 teaspoon salt
1 cup whole milk
2 1/2 cups warm water

In a bowl add 1/2 cup warm water, the yeast, half the corn meal, the salt and sugar and let set 5 minutes. Start to gradually add the flour and the water and mix well. When all the flour and water is mixed in, you'll begin to see a sticky dough has formed. In a bowl coated with oil, place the dough and cover. Allow to rise for 2 hours in a warm place.

Take a pinch of dough the size of a baseball and work it with your hands into an oblong. Place the oblong shaped dough on a cookie sheet lined with parchment paper. Flatten the oblong or oval shaped dough, and pinch the ends to form the Samoon shape. Cover with plastic and set aside in a warm place for another 2 hours.

Pour the milk in a small bowl. Flatten each Samoon dough again after it has risen and reshaped into Samoon. Score the top of the Samoon with a sharp knife. Brush the Samoon with milk, drenching the top and the sides of the Samoon dough.

Preheat oven to 450 degrees Fahrenheit. Place the oven racks in the top and bottom thirds of the oven. Fill a loaf pan with water and place it on the bottom rack.
Bake the bread approximately 12-15 minutes until golden brown. Place on a cooling rack.

Note-For crispier bread do not cover. If you want the Samoon to be soft and supple cover it in kitchen towels then when it has cooled, wrap in plastic bag. This bread is best served fresh.

Enjoy with Gemar or Harissa or anything you desire.

## Assyrian Lawasha

Many nationalities claim Lawasha originated with them. But that is a myth. The name of this bread is living proof that lawasha is an Assyrian word and invention. The word lawasha comes from the Assyrian word lesha, which means dough. The word lawasha simply means to open the dough, as we will be doing in this recipe.

Developing the yeast

2 1/4 teaspoons (1 packet) active dry yeast
1/2 cup warm water
1 teaspoon sugar
1/8 teaspoon salt
1 teaspoon vegetable oil

Combine the yeast, water, sugar, salt, and vegetable oil. Stir until the
yeast dissolves. Cover and let it sit for 30 minutes, until it becomes very foamy.

The dough

5 cups flour
1 teaspoon salt
2 teaspoons sugar
Developed yeast
3 tablespoons unsalted butter, melted
1 cup warm milk
3 tablespoons oil
1/2 cup warm water (divided in half)

Step 1-
While the khmira (yeast) is developing, sift together the flour, salt, and sugar into a big mixing bowl. Make a well in the center of the flour mixture and add the developed khmira, melted butter, milk, oil, and 1/4 cup of the water. Mix everything together with your hands until it starts to form a sticky ball. If the ball looks a little dry as it's coming together, add 1 tablespoon of the remaining water at a time until it's the right consistency. It should be sticky and soft, but it should form a ball as you knead it.

Knead the dough in the bowl, wetting your hands with additional water every minute or so if it looks a little dry. Knead by pulling the dough from the sides into the center of the ball and repeating. As you knead, the dough will start to become more elastic and will form a more cohesive ball. Continue to knead until it smooths out. Cover the bowl with plastic and put a blanket over it. Leave the dough to rise for 1 hour in a warm spot. The dough will double in size.

Opening the dough

Divide dough into 10 equal portions. Form each piece into a ball and place on a cookie sheet lined with parchment paper. Cover with plastic wrap and let the dough rise for another 45 minutes.

Preheat the oven to 500° F. Place each dough ball on a lightly floured surface and sprinkle a little flour on top. Use a rolling pin to roll it out into a large oval sheet with a thickness of about 1/8 inch. You should be able to see light through it when you hold it up.

Place the stretched dough on the back of a lightly greased cookie sheet, even the rims. Stretch the dough over the rims of the cookie sheet. With a fork poke holes into the sheet of dough to prevent bubbles. Bake the dough 2-5 minutes watching it carefully until golden. Remove from oven and place between towels so it doesn't dry out. If you want to turn it into a crispy cracker bread, allow it to dry out. Repeat with the remaining dough balls until all the sheets are cooked. To preserve the softness of the bread, store in a large plastic bag.

To rehydrate crispy bread simply sprinkle with a little bit of water and place it between towels for 10 minutes. Soft lawasha can be used for wraps and sandwiches, but it can also be dried to use for dips.

My nana Anna used to make lawasha and boushala all in the same day. She'd make stacks and stacks of Lawasha and would never cover them up. She'd let them dry out and stack them on a kitchen shelf. Mom did the same. Whenever we needed lawasha, mom would take one down, sprinkle it with water. Wrap it in towel and it would look and taste fresh.

**Assyrian Flat Bread**

3 cups flour
2 cups warm water
1 package or 2 1/2 teaspoons dry yeast
1 cup whole wheat flour
1 teaspoon salt

In a large bowl add 1/4 cup of warm water and the yeast. Mix and let rest for 5-8 minutes. Mix flour and salt together. Gradually start mixing the flour with the developed yeast and the rest of the warm water in the bowl and mix well till the dough is formed. You can use a dough mixer if you want. I like to knead the dough with my hands. Cover the dough and place in warm spot to let rise about 1 hour.

On a board sprinkle flour and put the dough on it. Divide the dough into six balls and place on parchment paper.  Sprinkle some flour on the board and using a rolling pin open each ball of dough into an oval shape. Place the opened oval dough on a greased cookie sheet. Pierce the oval dough with a fork all over. Bake in a preheated oven at 250 degrees Fahrenheit for 10-15 minutes or until golden on both sides. Don't let the bread brown.


**Assyrian Onion Bread**

1 spoon dry yeast,
1 cup hot water
2 teaspoons salt
3 cups flour
10 green onions
1 bunch de-stemmed, washed, strained and chopped parsley
1/2 cup melted butter

Mix the dry yeast with 1/4 cup warm water. Set aside for 30 minutes. Mix 3 cups flour, the yeast and the rest of water and mix well, kneading into a smooth dough. Cover with plastic and let rest 30 minutes.  Cut the dough in 4 pieces. Make each piece into a ball. And cover.

Chop the green onions and the parsley. Place them into a bowl. Add 1 teaspoon salt , 1 teaspoon oil and stir well. Cover with plastic.

On a well floured surface, open each dough ball into a paper thin sheet. Melt butter and spread all over the dough sheet. Place some of the onion mixture on top of the dough sheet spreading them out evenly. Roll one side of the dough all the way to the other end. Flatten the rolled out dough with your hand and begin to wrap it around itself, like a curled up snake. Do all four mounds of dough and place plastic wrap and cover for 20 minutes. Take one piece at a time and place on a cookie sheet lined with parchment paper. Press on it with your hands to open it and make it flatter and bigger. With a fork, pierce holes into the dough. Brush each one with milk. Bake for 30 minutes at 400 degrees Fahrenheit until golden.

## Assyrian Cheese bread-Takhratha

3 cups flour
2 cups crumbled Gupta (any cheese you like). I use Bulgarian Fetta, Chicago Cheese, or Kasseri, French Swiss cheese, or creamy Havarti, depending on my mood.
1 teaspoon sugar
1 envelop or one tablespoon dry yeast
1 teaspoon baking powder
1/4 cup oil
1 teaspoon Salt
1 cup warm water
1 minced onion
1 bunch parsley de-stemmed, washed and chopped
2 tablespoons butter
1/4 cup milk

Add the yeast and sugar to the warm water. Mix and set aside for 15 minutes.

Mix together the flour and oil with your hands until it forms into a crumble. Add the yeast mixture and mix well, kneading the dough until smooth and blended. Cover and let rise for 1 hour.
Separate the dough into 8 equal pieces. Form each piece into a ball. Cover and let rise again for 30-40 minutes.

In a sauce pan heat butter on high. Add the minced onion and sauté 2-3 minutes. Add the chopped parsley and sauté another 2-3. Place sautéed mixture into a bowl. Add the crumbled cheese and mix well.

Preheat oven to 400 degrees Fahrenheit

Take each dough piece and flatten it with your hands on a floured surface. Place 3-4 tablespoons of the cheese mixture on 1 side of the opened dough. Brush the edges with milk. Fold over the other side of the dough and close the Takhratha, pressing the dough edges together. It should look like a half moon. Crimp the ends to seal.

Place each Takhratha on a cookie sheet lined with parchment paper. Brush the tops with milk. Bake in the oven for 20-30 minutes or until the top is golden.

**ASSYRIAN ROASTS, FISH AND POULTRY**

**Mom's Masgoof-Assyrian Stuffed Fish**

My mother is famous for her Masgoof.

1 whole Carp Fish or any large white fish of your choice that has a similar texture.
Bass or Tilapia too, if you like.
1 bunch de-stemmed, washed and chopped parsley
1 minced onion
6 cloves crushed garlic
1 chopped tomato
3 tablespoons tomato sauce
1/4 cup curry powder
2 tablespoons fresh tamarind sauce
1 teaspoon salt
4 tablespoons olive oil
4-5 sliced tomatoes

Wash and pat dry the fish. Slit its belly and filet all the way to its spine. Lay the fish flat on its back (skin down) on a cookie sheet. Sprinkle a bit of salt and a bit of curry all over the fish.

In a bowl combine the minced onion, the chopped parsley, crushed garlic, the chopped tomato, the tomato sauce, the curry powder, the tamarind, the oil and the salt and mix well with your hands.

Spread the mixture all over the fish, covering the entire fish. Top with slices of tomatoes to cover the stuffing. Grill the fish in a grill basket for twenty minutes total, skin down.

You can also bake the fish in a preheated oven for 30 minutes at 375 degrees Fahrenheit, covered with aluminum paper. Remove aluminum foil and broil for 5 minutes.

Serve with your choice of rice and salad.

## Baghdad Masgoof

1 whole Carp Fish or any large white fish of your choice that has a similar texture. Bass or Tilapia is good too.

1 minced onion
2 bunches de-stemmed, washed and chopped parsley
6 cloves crushed garlic
2 chopped tomatoes
2 tablespoons tomato paste
1/4 cup curry powder
the juice of 1 lemon
1 tablespoon Tamarind sauce
1/2 teaspoon salt
4-5 sliced tomatoes
2 tablespoons butter
1/4 cup water

Wash and pat dry the fish. Butterfly the fish, (slit its belly and filet all the way to its spine). Lay the fish flat on its back (skin down) on a cookie sheet. Sprinkle the fish with salt and curry.

In a saucepan, melt the butter and add minced onion and crushed garlic. Sauté 2-3 minutes. Add the curry powder and sauté 1 minute. Add 1 chopped tomato, all the chopped parsley and sauté 2 minutes. Add the tomato paste and sauté 1 minute. Add the lemon juice, the tamarind sauce, the salt, the water. Mix well and simmer covered for 5 minutes. Allow mixture to cool 5 minutes.

Spread the mixture all over the fish. Top with sliced tomatoes. Cover the pan with aluminum and bake in a preheated oven for 30 minutes at 375 degrees Fahrenheit. Serve with rice and a nice salad.

In Iraq the fish is hung around a bon fire and cooked slow from the heat of the fire.

**Assyrian Baked Chicken**

Two whole chickens cut up into breasts, thighs, wings and drumsticks, or buy it already cut up. Wash the chicken well and strain in a colander. Pat the chicken dry with paper towels and place in a deep baking dish.

The marinade:
In a bowl or a large plastic bag with zipper combine:
1/2 cup oil
1/2 cup white vinegar
1/4 cup paprika
10 cloves crushed garlic
1 teaspoon salt
1/2 teaspoon black pepper
the zest of one lemon.

Place chicken in the marinade and zip up the bag. Or place chicken in a baking dish and pour the marinade all over it. Refrigerate for six hours and then turn the chicken pieces in the marinade and go to bed. If you have no time to marinate overnight, allow it to marinade at least 2 hours.

Place the contents of the plastic bag into the baking dish, (chicken and the marinade together). If you've marinated the chicken in a baking dish, place the dish in a preheat oven at 400 degrees Fahrenheit. Bake the chicken covered for 40 minutes. Remove cover and bake another 30 minutes.

Usually this is served with dill and Fava beans rice and a nice salad of your choice.

**Assyrian Stuffed chicken and Rice**

1 whole chicken
4 cups Basmati rice soaked for 30 minutes
1/2 cup vermicelli
1 cup blanched and peeled almonds
1/2 cup golden raisins
1 tablespoon baharat
1 1/2 teaspoon curry powder
1 1/2 teaspoon cumin powder
1 1/2 teaspoon ground cloves
1 1/2 teaspoon ground cardamom
3 tablespoons saffron oil or 1 teaspoon Saffron threads soaked in 1/4 cup hot water
1/4 cup orange blossom water
8 cloves crushed garlic
1 stick of butter softened

1/2 cup oil
1 tablespoons salt
1/4 teaspoon black pepper
1 1/2 sticks butter

Trim all excess fat from chicken and rinse well. Place in a colander to drain.

In a bowl combine all spices, (1 teaspoons curry powder, 1 teaspoon cumin powder, 1 teaspoon ground cloves, 1 teaspoon cardamom). Add 1 stick softened butter, the crushed garlic and orange blossom and mix well. Place the chicken in a roasting pan and sprinkle the chicken with salt inside and out. Rub the butter and spice mixture all over the chicken inside and out and set aside.

In a large sauce pan add 1 1/2 stick of butter and melt on high heat. Add the vermicelli, the blanched almonds and sauté a few minutes until the mixture turns golden brown. Add the strained rice and sauté 2-3 minutes.

Add the raisins and sauté 1 minute. Add 1/2 teaspoon curry, 1/2 teaspoon ground cloves, 1/2 teaspoon ground cumin powder, 1/2 teaspoon cardamom powder, 1 teaspoon saffron threads, 1 tablespoon baharat and 2 tablespoons orange blossom and sauté 1 minute.

Add 6 cups water, 1 tablespoon salt and bring to boil. When most of the liquid is evaporated, turn flame to low, cover the pan and simmer for 30 minutes.

When the rice is cooked, allow to cool for 30 minutes. Then spoon as much of the rice mixture into the chicken cavity as you can fit. Tie the chicken legs together with thread. Place the chicken pan in a preheated oven at 350 degrees Fahrenheit. Roast the chicken covered for 1 1/2 hours, basting with the liquid. Remove the cover and brown the chicken in the oven for 20-30 minutes.

Place the chicken on a platter and add the remaining rice all around it.

## Assyrian Roast Beef or Lamb

1 Rump Roast
1/4 cup oil
6 cloves sliced garlic
2 tablespoons bahart
1 teaspoon salt
1/2 teaspoon black pepper

Wash the roast and pat dry. With a knife poke holes all over the roast top, sides and bottom. Drizzle with oil. Sprinkle with salt all over the roast. Now rub the roast with baharat all over. Take each sliced garlic and put it into the holes you created with a knife. If you're baking in the oven, cover it and bake at 350 degrees Fahrenheit for 2 hours.

Instead of the oven, I usually use a crock pot to cook my roast. Turn the crockpot to high. Place the roast fat side up. Cover the crockpot. Allow this to cook at least 3-4 hours, occasionally turning upside down to drench in the juices.

**Assyrian Dobo Tur Abdin Style**
This recipe was contributed by Gaby and Elizabeth Gabriel. He writes:

The preparation of Dobo the Assyrian traditional dish from Tur-Abdin( in today's) Turkey.

Dobo can be prepared according to each individual taste by adding more or less salt as needed, Tomato paste, Black pepper, Hot Chili, Capsicum paste or whatever each individual wish to add to it.

The Lamb
1 Lamb leg
10 cloves sliced garlic
10 cloves black pepper corn
1/4 cup oil
3 tablespoons tomato paste
12 cups of water
1 teaspoon salt

Clean and remove the excess fat from the leg of lamb. Brush some oil on the leg. Sprinkle with salt all over. With the tip of the knife poke holes into the leg top, bottom, and the edges.  Stuff as much as needed garlic cloves and black pepper corn into the holes.

In a large pan add the rest of the oil and heat on high. Sauté the lamb leg until it's brown on all sides. Add 10 cups of water to the lamb pan and bring to boil. Add 3 tablespoons of tomato paste and stir well to dissolve the paste. Cover and simmer 2 hours until the lamb is tender. Reserve 4 cups of broth for the bulgar.

The preparation of Bulgur cooked with the broth of the Dobo.

4 cups premixed bulgar # 4 with sha'aria (vermicelli)
2 tablespoons butter or margarine or oil
1 teaspoon salt

In a pan, heat 2 tablespoons butter or margarine or oil. Add the Bulgur and sauté until lightly toasted. Add 4 cups of the Dobo liquid you reserved, and 1/2 teaspoon salt. Stir well, cover and bring to boil. When the broth is nearly all evaporated, reduce heat and simmer until Bulgar is soft and fluffy.

Serve the Bulgur with Dobo (leg of lamb)


## Assyrian Quzzi

Make Mom's Biryani by following the recipe on page 52. It goes very well with this dish.

The Lamb Roasting:
2 boneless legs of lamb (ask the butcher to do it)
8 cloves crushed garlic
4 tablespoons baharat
1/2 teaspoon turmeric
1 teaspoon ground cloves
1 teaspoon ground cardamom
1 teaspoon ground cumin
1 teaspoon ground cinnamon
1/4 cup rose water
1 tablespoon tamarind
1 teaspoon salt
1/4 teaspoon black pepper
1 stick butter softened
1/2 stick butter for searing the lamb
1 pot of Mom's biryani
1/2 stick melted butter
In a bowl add all dry spices together and mix well. Add the crushed garlic and softened butter, tamarind sauce and rose water and mix into a paste. Rub the mixture all over the deboned lamb and refrigerate for 1 hour.

Preheat oven at 300 degrees Fahrenheit.

In a large skillet add 1/2 half stick butter and melt. Add the lamb to the skillet and sear on both sides. Remove from heat and set aside to cool. When the lamb is cool to the touch, lay one of the seared leg of lamb flat in a big roasting pan. place 4-5 cups of mom's Biryani over it. Add the second seared lamb on top of the rice Biryani. Sew together all sides of the lamb closed with either needle and thread or roasting pins. Bake covered for 2 1/2 hours.

Uncover and add melted butter all over the lamb and bake another 1/2 hour. Place the lamb in the center of a big platter. Remove all thread and pins. Add more Biryani all around it.

## ASSYRIAN TOURSHI-Pickles

Below photo I took at the market in Baghdad from my last trip to the homeland

My Tourshi after marinating for 1 week

## Assyrian Tourshi

The Vegetables:
1 Cauliflower head, washed and cut to small florets
25 pickling cucumbers, cut 1 inch in size
10 carrots washed and cut into 2-inch pieces
10 stalks of celery washed and cut into 2-inch pieces
1 pound green beans, washed and cut into 2-inch pieces
1/2 bunch Parsley washed
1 pound Jerusalem artichokes (Khaboosha d'Ara'a)
1 large jar Persian garlic, sliced (Thoom Ajam)
1 pound pickled pepperoncinis
1 cup green, cured olives
1/2 cabbage (leaves sliced 2 inches each)

In a large bowl combine all raw vegetables and mix them well. Begin to put all the mixed vegetables half way full in large jars with lids.

The Pickling Liquid:

8 cups of apple Cider Vinegar
6 cups water
1 cup sea salt
1 cup chopped garlic
1/2 cup pickling curry powder. If unavailable use regular curry powder
1 tablespoon turmeric


In a large pot combine salt and water and stir to dissolve. Bring to boil for 5 minutes. Add the vinegar, the garlic and the turmeric, the curry powder and bring to boil again. Reduce heat and simmer for 1 hour, covered. Take cover off and allow to cool to lukewarm.

With a large ladle, spoon the pickling liquid over the jarred vegetables. Leave an inch of space to the top of the jar. Seal the lid and allow the pickles to marinate for 3-4 days before refrigerating them. After 4 days place the pickles in the refrigerator until all the pickles are consumed.

**Tourshi d'Silqa-Red beet Tourshi (Moukhalalat)**

4 turnips (Shalgham) washed and peeled
2 red beets (shwandar) washed and peeled
4 cups water
1/2 cup white vinegar
1/4 cup iodized salt

Peel and slice all turnips and beets. For each 2 sliced turnips we need 1 sliced beet.
Put into jars, mixing the two.

Combine 4 cups water, 1/2 cup vinegar and the salt and mix well. Poor over the
jarred vegetables. Seal the lid and allow the pickles to marinade. During this process,
the turnips will turn pinkish red. Now you can refrigerate and use as needed.

## Assyrian Stuffed Tourshi

3 cups water
2 cups apple cider vinegar
1/4 cup salt

In a big pot, add all ingredients, mix well and bring to boil for 10 minutes. Set aside.

10 Japanese Eggplants washed and pricked with a toothpick
10 peppers of any kind you like, washed.
30 pickling cucumbers washed

Cut off the ends of the cucumbers and eggplants.  Place into a large jar along with all the peppers and the parsley. With a ladle, spoon the cooked vinegar over them and seal the jar with a tight lid. Refrigerate for a week.

Remove the pickled vegetables from the pickling jar, discard the pickling liquid. With a sharp knife, slit all of them, except 4 pickles to reserve for the stuffing.

The Stuffing
2 bunches parsley chopped (save the stems)
1 carrot shredded
20 cloves chopped garlic
1/4 cup curry powder
2 tablespoons olive oil for each jar
4 chopped pickled cucumbers

Mix well and set aside.

The pickling juice:
10 cups water
8 cups Apple Cider vinegar
1/4 cup salt
1/2 cup pickling curry or curry powder
20 cloves crushed garlic

In a large pot mix the water with the salt and stir well. Bring to boil. Add the vinegar, and curry powder and bring to boil again for 10 minutes. Add the sliced garlic and reduce heat to low and let simmer for 1 hour.

While you're waiting for the mixture to cook well, stuff the pickles.

Slit all the pickles in the middle, not on the ends. Spoon some stuffing inside the slit and tie with the parsley stems. Put all stuffed pickles back into the jar.

Cool the pickling juice to lukewarm. With a ladle, spoon the mixture into the jar of the stuffed pickles, leaving 1 inch space to the top. Add 2 tablespoons of olive oil to each jar. Seal the lids and store in a cool garage or storage room for 3-4 days. After that store in a refrigerator to last you all year.

## ASSYRIAN BREAKFAST/BRUNCH

### Assyrian Sunday Omelette

6 eggs whipped
2 tablespoons whole milk
1 minced onion
2 green sweet chili peppers chopped
1 tomato chopped
1/4 cup chopped cilantro
1 teaspoon salt
1/2 teaspoon black pepper
1/4 cup oil

In a pan add the oil and heat on high. Add minced onions and chopped pepper and sauté 3-5 minutes until onion are translucent. Add chopped tomato and sauté 1-2 minutes. Add half the salt and stir.

In a bowl whip the eggs with 2 tablespoons milk and the rest of the salt. Add the chopped cilantro. Pour egg mixture all over the sautéed vegetables. Reduce heat to very low. Cover the pan and do not disturb the omelette until cooked. You'll know it's cooked when you shake the pan and the eggs don't run all over the place, but stay firm and solid.

Serve with lawasha or Samoon and chai.

**Assyrian Speera-Omelette**

6 eggs
1 minced onion
1/2 bunch flat leaf parsley de-stemmed, washed and chopped
1 teaspoon salt
1/2 teaspoon black pepper
1/4 cup oil

In a large pan, heat the oil on high. Add 1 minced onion and half the salt. Mix and sauté 3-5 minutes.

In a bowl whip the eggs with 2 tablespoons milk. Add the chopped parsley, the rest of salt and all the black pepper. Mix well and pour over the sautéed onions. Turn heat to low, cover the pan and simmer until eggs are cooked solid.

**BEETA ILLIKH-Soft Boiled Eggs**

1-Boil the eggs in the shell 3-4 minutes. Place the egg in the egg holder. Crack the top with a spoon. Removed the top, creating a hole. Dip your spoon into the egg and scrape some cooked egg white dipped in yolk.

Alternative:
In a small sauce pan, 1/4 of the way filled with water add 1/2 teaspoon salt and a cap full of white vinegar and bring to boil. Turn down heat to low. Crack an egg into the water and cover the saucepan. Do not disturb for 3 minutes. Lift the lid to check if the egg is still runny around the yolk. If it is, give it another 1-2 minutes. The cooking of the egg should not exceed 5 minutes from the time you drop the eggs into the water. Remove and drain well with a slotted spoon and place into a bowl. With a fork, mash the eggs and add salt and pepper to taste. Serve with toast or Samoon interchangeably.

# Gozlama

The Dough:
3 cups flour
1 1/4 cups warm water
1 packet dry yeast
1 spoon sugar
2 tablespoons olive oil
1/2 cup yogurt

In a small bowl combine yeast, warm water and sugar and set aside for the yeast to develop.

Sift the flour into a mixing bowl and add the salt and 2 tablespoons oil. Mix well. Add the developed yeast mixture and the yogurt and work into a smooth dough. If the dough doesn't pull away from the bowl, add more flour and keep kneading. Divide the dough into 6 balls. Cover with a clean cloth and let rise for 20-30 minutes.

Place a plastic on a smooth surface and grease the plastic. Place each dough ball onto the greased plastic. With a rolling pin, roll out each dough ball into a paper thin sheet.

The Filling: You can fill the Gozlama with anything you want. This one is a vegetarian

1 bunch chopped spinach
1 bunch chopped parsley
1 minced onion
1 bunch Kawar (chives) chopped
5 cloves crushed garlic
1 tablespoon smoked paprika
1 teaspoon ground cumin
1 teaspoon ground coriander seeds
1/4 cup chopped mint
1 cup feta cheese
1/2 teaspoon salt
1/4 teaspoon black pepper
4 tablespoons butter

In a frying pan melt the butter. Add the the onions and garlic and sauté 2-3 minutes. Add all the spices including salt and pepper and sauté 2-3 minutes. Add all the herbs and sauté 3-5 minutes. Allow the stuffing to cool before filling the Gozlama.

Open each dough ball into thin sheets. Fill one side of the dough with stuffing and spread evenly. Fold the other side over and seal the dough edges using water. Brush with oil. In a dry frying pan, cook the Gozlama on medium heat till golden brown. Flip to other side and cook till golden brown. You now can cut the Gozlama into pieces and serve with Masta Tooma.

**Jean Yonan's famous Spinach Omellete**
Mom made this for us every Sunday. It's her signature breakfast

6 eggs beaten
2 tablespoons whole milk
2 bags of spinach or one large bunch, de-stemmed, washed and chopped.
1 large onion sliced thin
5 cloves garlic sliced thin
1 teaspoon salt
1/2 teaspoon pepper
1/4 cup oil

In a large frying pan add all the chopped spinach and slowly stir until it is wilted and starting to form liquid in the pan. Strain the spinach in a colander and press with a large spoon to squeeze the water out.

In the same large frying pan, add 1/4 cup oil and coat the pan on high heat. Add the onions and garlic and sauté until golden, 3-5 minutes. Add the strained spinach and half the salt and sauté another 2-3 minutes.

In a bowl beat the eggs with 2 tablespoons milk. Add the rest of the salt and all the black pepper. Mix well and pour over the sautéed vegetables. Cover the pan and reduce heat to low and let the eggs cook solid.

Enjoy with lawasha.


**Beeta Qleeta d'Badimjaneh smooqeh-Fried Eggs and Tomatoes**

6 eggs
4 tomatoes sliced
1/4 cup oil or 1/2 stick butter

In a large frying pan heat 1/2 stick of butter or oil. Place the tomatoes in the hot oil and fry on both sides. Reduce heat and crack six eggs over the tomatoes. Cover the lid and let the eggs cook on low heat. Sprinkle with salt and pepper.

Enjoy with lawasha or your favorite bread

## Beeta d'Qirtopeh-Egg and Potato Skillet Pie

3 peeled and diced potatoes
1 diced onion
1 diced sweet green pepper
1 diced tomato
6 eggs
1/4 cup oil
1 tablespoon paprika
1/2 teaspoon salt
1/4 teaspoon black pepper

In a skillet, heat oil on high. Add the diced potatoes and sauté 4-5 minutes. Add the onions and peppers and sauté 2-3 minutes. Add the paprika and sauté 1 minute, stirring well. Add the diced tomato and sauté 1 minute. Add the salt and pepper and stir well. Reduce heat to low. Crack the eggs over the potato mixture. Sprinkle the eggs with a pinch of salt and pepper. When the eggs are no longer runny, slice the pie and serve in a plate.

Enjoy with your favorite kind of bread


## Gillaleh (herb) Omelette

4 large eggs
2 tablespoon milk
1/2 cup chopped Parsley
1/2 cup chopped dill
1/2 cup chopped Cilantro
1/2 cup chopped green onions
4 cloves crushed garlic
2 tablespoons flour
1/4 teaspoon black pepper
1/2 teaspoon salt
1/2 stick butter

In a bowl, beat the eggs, salt, pepper, and flour. Add all chopped herbs and whisk to combine. In a frying pan, add the butter and heat on medium. Add the chopped onions and garlic and sauté 2-3 minutes. Add the whisked egg mixture all over the onions. Immediately cover the pan and reduce heat. Allow omelette to set solid. Remove from heat and serve.

## Gemar-Assyrian Qishdda-Assyrian Breakfast Cream

In Assyria Gemar is made with Buffalo milk, (Jamoose). This is not widely available in America or anywhere in the Diaspora.

8 cups Heavy whipping cream
8 cups whole milk

Pour the milk and the cream into a large pot. Heat on medium heat for 20 minutes. Do not boil. When the milk foam starts to rise, remove from heat and place the pot on the counter. Put a mesh sieve or a colander over the pot. Place a towel over the sieve. Place a very heavy blanket over the towel. Leave to rest for 6-8 hours in a warm place. Place the pot in the fridge for 5 days. Take the pot out and with a knife, release the edges. With a flat ladle, reach under the cream and take the solidified and firm cream and place in a deep dish. Do that to each layer you remove, stacking the Gemar. Serve the Gemar chilled.

Enjoy with Samoon, your favorite jam and chai for breakfast. Refrigerate the rest.


## Assyrian Qishdda-Breakfast cream

4 cups whipping cream
4 cups whole milk
1/4 cup corn starch

In a large bowl mix the three very well and transfer to a pan. Heat over high flame stirring constantly. Do not stop stirring until the milk mixture thickens. Pour the milk mixture into a deep dish. Allow to cool before placing in the refrigerator.

If you want to make a smaller portion of qishdda:
1 pint whipping cream
2 tablespoons corn starch

In a small bowl mix 1/2 cup cream and 2 tablespoons starch. Mix well until blended and smooth. Add the rest of the cream into a saucepan. Add the corn starch mixture and mix well. Heat over medium heat constantly stirring. When the mixture thickens pour into a deep dish and let it cool for a few hours and turn into a mold. With a spatula cut length wise into three different sections. With the same spatula, begin to scrape and push the qishdda from one end of the tray to the other. The qishdda will start to fold as you push the spatula to gather it. Place each gathered section in a plate and enjoy. Refrigerate the unused portion for later use.

Serve with Samoon and jam and enjoy with chai.

**Takhin and Nepookhta-Tahini and Molasses**

Assyrians love to eat tahini and date molasses with a Samoon for breakfast.
Stir the Tahini jar well to mix the separated tahini from the oil. Spoon the tahini on half of the plate. Spoon date molasses on the other half of the plate. Eat with Samoon and enjoy with chai.

**Assyrian Jajik**

1 pint small curd cottage cheese
1/2 stick butter chopped finely
2 tablespoons sour creme
1/2 bunch dill de-stemmed, washed and chopped
1/2 bunch cilantro de-stemmed, washed and chopped
1/2 bunch chives washed and chopped
optional-1 small hot pepper chopped
1/4 teaspoon salt

In a bowl combine all ingredients and mix well. Place the jajik in a container with lid and refrigerate. Enjoy with Lawasha or Samoon and some chai.

**Assyrian Basturma**

1 pound extra lean beef roast
1 tablespoon salt
3 tablespoons ground Fenugreek seeds
3 tablespoons paprika
1 tablespoon black pepper
1 tablespoon garlic powder
1 tablespoon baharat
1 tablespoon cumin powder
1 cup warm water
2 cloth bags or large cone coffee filters
3 cups salt for curing the beef

Slice the roast in half, length wise. Wash both pieces and pat dry with paper towels. Wrap again in a kitchen cloth towel and let stand for 10 minutes for the liquid to be absorbed.

In a cookie sheet place a layer of salt. Place the beef pieces one a time in the salt and completely cover the beef with salt on all sides. Put the beef in cloth bags or coffee filters and hang in a dry cold place, like a storage room or basement. If neither are available hang them in the fridge. After 5-6 days, wash the beef well, scraping any remaining salt. Pat dry the beef.

In a bowl combine all the spices, salt and garlic power and mix well. Gradually add water and mix well to blend smoothly, to make it like a paste. Rub the paste all over the meat making sure every inch of it is covered. Hang again in a cool dry place for 3 weeks. Keep the meat refrigerated when not using and only slice what you need.

Enjoy with fried eggs


## Assyrian beef Basturma sausage

1 pound extra lean ground beef
10 cloves crushed garlic
1 teaspoon salt
1 teaspoon black pepper
1 tablespoon baharat
1 tablespoon cumin powder

1 pound of cleaned and washed cow intestines or long fiber casings for stuffing.

In a bowl, mix all ingredients and refrigerate overnight. Stuff the intestines with the mixture. Tie the ends of intestines into knots. With a sharp knife poke holes into the intestines. With a rolling pin flatten out. Hang in a dry but cold place, like a storage room or a cold garage, or even refrigerator for 2 weeks.

When ready to use, peel off the casing. Slice the basturma into thin slices.

In a pan, melt butter, fry an egg and some basturma an enjoy with lawasha or Samoon.

## DURMAK-ASSYRIAN SANDWICHES

From as long as I can remember I did not enjoy sitting at the table with my family and eating lunch or dinner. The reason for this was that I despised the smell and taste of lamb. In the Middle East that's what's mostly available. Cattle is scarce and the cow is used for milking only and the milk in turn is used to make dairy products. So you can imagine how hellish the meals were for me. For that reason I was a vegetarian until the age of 12 when we moved to the USA.

Once we arrived in Morton Grove, Illinois, mom started buying beef so I could eat meat. I began enjoying meals with my family because there was no awful smell or taste in the food.

For the first 12 years of my life I lived on sandwiches of any kind without meat, such as hardboiled eggs, Amba and tomato sandwiches, and falafel sandwiches. Now, in my old age I still love sandwiches of any kind; beef kabob, meatball sandwich, cutleteh sandwiches or any vegan or vegetarian sandwich.

### Cutleteh Sandwich

To make the Cutleteh follow the recipe in this book.

Open a Samoon or French roll and put tomato slices, cutleteh, and gillaleh and enjoy. You can use lawasha to make a wrap out of it too.

### Falafel Sandwich

To make Falafels and tahini sauce, follow the recipes in this book.

Open a Samoon and fill with Falafel, sliced or diced tomatoes, onions, lettuce and whatever else you like. I like this sandwich without tahini because this is how we eat it in Iraq, but you can drizzle tahini sauce all over it. See the tahini garlic sauce recipe under falafel. You can use lawasha or pita bread to make this sandwich too.

**Mom's Biyeh Shleeqeh Durmak**-Hard boiled egg sandwich

Open a Samoon and fill with sliced and salted hard boiled eggs, sliced and salted tomatoes, sliced pickled mangos (Amba), green onions and a handful of toleh (Cilantro) or Parsley, depending on your taste. You can make this sandwich using lawasha to wrap or pita pocket.


**Shawarma Sandwich**

Open a Samoon, a lawasha or pita bread and fill with chicken or beef shawarma, onions, tomatoes, and tourshi. You can also drizzle tahini sauce on it


**Amba Sandwich**

Open a Samoon and fill with Amba, sliced tomatoes, and lots of Cilantro, water cress, and green onions. Enjoy with tourshi


**Baked or roasted chicken Sandwich**

Open a Samoon and spread some hummus on both sides. Fill with slices of baked or roasted, or Rotisseri chicken, tomatoes, onions, Cilantro. Enjoy with Tourshi.


**Basturma Sandwich**

Slice some Basturma and tomatoes and fry on both sides in some butter or oil. Place the fried Basturma and tomatoes inside the sandwich and enjoy.

**Kipteh Sandwich**

Spoon some Kipteh sauce and 1 Kipteh ball and warm them up in a bowl. Slightly mash the kipteh with a fork. Place the Kipteh and the sauce inside an open Samoon and fill with gillaleh, especially basil, green onions and enjoy.


**Taboulla Sandwich**

Make some Taboula from the recipe in this cook book. Open a Samoon and fill with Taboula. Enjoy this vegan sandwich with Some tourshi.

## Kabob Sandwich

Follow the recipes in this book to make sheesh kabob, or chicken tikka or beef tikka and vegetable kabob. Open a Samoon and spread some of the vegetable kabob on both sides of the bread. Place the kabob inside the bread and sprinkle with Sumac. Fill the sandwich with sliced onions and gillaleh and enjoy.

## Chilli Fry Sandwich-

Open the Samoon and fill with chillifry. Add handfuls of gillaleh and enjoy.

## Dolma Sandwich

Take one sheet of lawasha and fill it with any kind of dolma. Wrap it and enjoy.

## Qeemah Sandwich

Open a Samoon and fill with qeemah. Add a hand full of gillaleh, especially cilantro and green onions and enjoy

## ASSYRIAN BEVERAGES

### Watermelon Juice
Discard the green rind/peel of 6 slices of watermelon. Place the watermelon in a blender and on low speed, process until blended. Strain through a mesh sieve. Pour over ice and enjoy

### Cherry Juice
2 cups washed and pitted cherries blended and strained to remove the skin. Pour in a glass over ice and enjoy.

### Lemonade
Cut 4 lemons in half and juice with a citrus juicer. Strain the pulp and add the lemon to a glass. Add water to the lemon juice and simple syrup. Mix well and enjoy a glass over ice, with a sprig of mint.

Simple syrup
1 cup water
2 cups sugar
1 tablespoon lemon juice

Bring sugar and water to boil for 10 minutes. Add lemon and stir. Remove from heat and cool.

### Pomegranate Juice
2 large pomegranates or 4 small ones. Pound each pomegranate against a hard surface or the kitchen counter until soft and supple to your touch. Core out the stem and Insert a metal straw where the stem was. Enjoy slurping it with a straw or cut the pomegranates in half and squeeze all the juice out. Pour into a glass over ice and enjoy.

### Date Drink
Soak 5-6 pitted dates in a cup of water for 1 hour. Pour into a blender and blend well. Strain through a mesh sieve to remove the skin. Pour into a glass and mix with 1 tablespoon lemon juice. Stir well and enjoy over ice

### Tamar Hindi drink
Peel 4 pods of Tamarind and soak for a few hours. Stir and breakdown with a fork separating the seeds and the stems from the pulp. Discard the stems and seeds. Pour the soaked pulp through a mesh sieve. Pour the filtered tamarind pulp into a bowl. Gradually add water and stir until blended. Taste the drink to see if you want it weaker to add more water. Add some sugar and taste again. If it is too sour, add more sugar. Pour some into a glass and enjoy over ice. You can spice it up by adding cayenne or any hot chili and mix well.

**Plain Daweh-Doogh**
In a bowl, beat 4-5 tablespoons of plain yogurt until smoothly blended. Gradually add water and beat till smooth. Add a pinch of salt and stir well. Enjoy ice cold.


**Mint Daweh-Doogh**
Make the above plain Daweh and add dry or fresh mint and stir well. Strain through a mesh sieve to remove all the mint. Add a pinch of salt. Enjoy ice cold


**Mango Yogurt Drink**
In a blender combine some peeled and sliced ripe mangoes and yogurt. Blend on high speed. Chill and serve in a glass. Add sugar or honey to taste


**Pomegranate Yogurt Drink**
Combine 2 tablespoons of pomegranate syrup with 4 tablespoons yogurt, 1/2 cup water. Blend well and chill. Pour into a glass and enjoy.


**Sherbet**-Assyrians love sherbet. These are different kinds of syrups, such as orange, sour cherry, pomegranate, etc. We mix a few spoonfuls of the sherbet with water and stir well. Pour into a glass over ice and enjoy.

**Assyrian Simowar Chai**

In a grill, light up some charcoal. Wait till the flame dies down a bit. Place the charcoal inside the Simowar charcoal tube. Fill the Simowar belly with hot water and let it come to a boil.

In a metal teapot, place 4-5 tablespoons of loose black tea. Fill the tea pot with boiling water from the Simowar. Place the teapot on top of the charcoal tube. Allow for the tea to brew (shaqil dem). When the tea is brewed, pour a little tea from the teapot into a tea glass or cup and fill the rest with boiling water from the Simowar. Enjoy the Simowar tea with Dishlama, a cooked sugar cube Assyrians make.

**Stove top Chai-**

Fill the kettle with water. Place on high heat and bring to boil. In a teapot add 4-5 tablespoons loose black tea. When the water boils, fill the tea pot with boiling water. Place the lid on the teapot and cook for 20 seconds on high heat. Remove from heat and place the teapot over the kettle. Keep the flame on low to keep the hot temperature of the water. Pour some tea from the teapot into a tea glass or cup. Fill the rest of the cup with boiling water. Enjoy hot with a Dishlama.

**Qahwa-Assyrian coffee**

Assyrians of Iraq cook the coffee with water, but Persian Assyrians like to cook the coffee with milk.

Most Assyrians buy finely ground coffee already mixed. You can ask the mix to be half light and half dark beans. You can also ask the coffee to be mixed with hail (cardamom).

I don't like any premixed coffee. I like to buy French Roast beans and grind my own coffee in a grinder.

However you like it, the technique of making Assyrian coffee is the same. If you're making 3 cups of qahwa, use three cups of water and 3 heaping teaspoons of finely ground coffee. If you like it bitter, don't use sugar. But for each two teaspoons of coffee, I add 1 teaspoon of sugar.

The ratio for making two cups is: 2 qahwa cups water, 2 heaping teaspoons of finely ground coffee, 1 teaspoon sugar. Combine all three in a qahwadan and cook over high heat and stir well to make sure there are no lumps. Bring to boil and immediately remove from heat before the foam spills all over the stove. Pour into small cups and enjoy with a date.

Back in the homeland housewives took an afternoon break and came together to have qahwa, similar to a coffee clutch in America.

## ASSYRIAN ALCOHOLIC BEVERAGES

Beer was invented in ancient Assyria. Clay tablets attest to the fact that we had a goddess of Beer and the Beer recipe was made into a prayer that everyone was expected to recite lest anyone forgot the recipe.

Assyrians also make their own wine, date Arak and grape Arak, (a clear distilled alcohol that when mixed with water turns cloudy.) This is poured over a glass of ice and enjoyed with some Mezzas (appetizers). When I was a kid back home, dad would play tawlee (backgammon) with his friends after dinner. He'd make the Arak drinks and ask me to make them Mezzas. I only knew how to make sliced cucumbers and sliced tomatoes placed on a plate, sprinkled with salt and garnished with olives. But dad loved this mezza and always asked me to make it for him and his friends. I wish I could do that for him now.

**Assyrian Wine-**Assyrians made wines in the Urmia, Hikkari, Nineveh and the Tur Abdin regions of Assyria

Just as there are over a hundred variety of dates in Assyria, the Assyrians cultivated approximately 1200 variety of grapes. Most notably were their single vineyard grape wines, which they would use to make estate wines. They cost a lot more than the varietal grape wine. The tannins in their wines were a bit stronger than French wines or today's California wines, but because the soil was exceptional for grape growing, the Assyrian wines were considered much finer than any Western-made wines and would naturally pick up the fruity or the peppery taste from the soil.

The Assyrians terraced their vineyards to stretch the season for grape growing. The grapes grown on the plains of Assyria would ripen much earlier than the hillside grown grapes. So we not only had grapes most of the year, but each vineyard had a different tasting grape, depending on the sugars formed in the grapes, and the tannins produced from the stems.

The other difference was Assyrian wines were fermented in qadaleh (clay jars) whereas the Western wines are fermented in metal containers then stored in Oak barrels to obtain those flavors that you get from aged oak.

# MECHANICAL FOOD

Feeding Toddlers and the Elderly

When my son was an infant he was breastfed. But when he turned 14 months I began feeding him Assyrian mechanical food, which I would either mash with a fork or blend in a blender.

When my father got sick I learned how to make him mechanical food all over again. I am currently the sole care taker of my mom for 8 years now. As she began to decline and chewing was exhausting for her and swallowing even more difficult, I started making her mechanical food too.

Some of the more nutritious mechanical foods are:

Always have some beef or chicken broth on hand to add to the following:

In a pot, pour 2 cups of bone broth, 1/2 chicken breast chopped, 1/2 an onion chopped, a handful of spinach chopped, 1 chopped zucchini and bring to boil. Reduce heat and let simmer for 30 minutes. Add salt to taste. Blend the soup and feed with a spoon or syringe.

-Dolma-Take the leaves off, mix it with masta tooma and mash with a fork until it's mushy. Feed with a baby spoon. When the elder begins to decline, blend the dolma and masta tooma with a little beef broth and feed it to them with a large syringe.

-Chicken and rice-Make rizza zardeh with peas and carrots. In a sauce pan, cook 1/2 of a chopped chicken breast and 1 cup bone broth. Bring to boil and reduce heat and simmer on low, covered. When the chicken is thoroughly cooked, combine the chicken with 1/2 cup of cooked rice and blend. You can always add more broth if it's too thick for them. Feed with a spoon or a large syringe.

-Beef barley soup-In a blender, blend two cups of soup. Pour into a bowl and heat and feed with a spoon or a large syringe.

-Creamy chicken and Rice Soup-This is delicious, nutritious and easy to feed to toddlers and elderly if you mince all the vegetables and the chicken. You can blend it too to make it easier.

-Salisbury steak and mashed potatoes-Take 2 salisbury stakes and blend with 1/4 cup gravy and 1/4 cup beef broth. Pour over a bowl of mashed potatoes and feed with a spoon. As the elder declines add more broth to this combination and blend with the mashed potatoes and feed with a spoon or a large syringe.

-Kubba Hamouth-Place 3 kubbas and 1 cup of the sauce and blend in a blender. Feed with a spoon or a large syringe.

-Any Shirwa and Rizza -1/2 cup cooked rice and 1 cup cooked shirwa. Blend in a blender and feed with a spoon or syringe.

-Grilled or baked chicken and rice-blend 1/2 cup rice and one piece of cooked chicken, with a 1/4-1/2 cup chicken broth. Feed with a spoon or large syringe.

-Harissa-Blend 2 cups of Harissa. If it's too pasty add some broth to make it soupy. Feed with a spoon or syringe.

-Kipteh-Blend one meatball of kipteh and 1 cup of the sauce. Feed with spoon or syringe.

-Any soup-Blend 2 cups of any kind of soup and feed with a spoon or a syringe

-Any hot cereal, especially oatmeal- Once the oatmeal is cooked, add 1 tablespoon butter, some honey and 2 tablespoons milk. Mix well and feed.

-Mixed vegetables-Cook mixed vegetables with a little broth and blend. Feed with a spoon or syringe

-Kabob and Rice-Blend 1/2 cup rice with 1 ground beef kabob, or 1/2 cup chicken tikka or beef tikka, and 1/2 cup broth of any kind. Heat and feed with spoon or syringe.


-Beeta Illikh-Soft boiled eggs (great source of protein and great for the brain for those with dementia)-See my recipe for Beeta Illikh. Mash the eggs with a fork and feed with a tea spoon.

-Beeta qleeta-Fried eggs (over easy)-Fry 2 eggs and mash with a fork. Feed with a spoon.

-Avocado-This is a good source of protein and good LDL (cholesterol). Mash one avocado in a bowl. Add a pinch of salt, 1 tablespoon lemon juice, 2 cloves crushed garlic. Mash with a fork and feed as a side dish to eggs or a nice snack.

## Smoothies

Banana and strawberry smoothie-Blend 1 peeled banana, 5 washed and de-stemmed strawberries with a 1/2 cup of milk. Feed with a spoon or syringe

Spinach smoothie-blend a handful of spinach, 1/2 an avocado, 1 banana, 2 tablespoons protein powder. Feed with a spoon or syringe

Kale smoothie-Blend a handful of kale, 1 cluster grapes, 1 banana, 1 small container of yogurt or Activia, 1/2 cup milk. Strain through a metal mesh colander to remove grape skins. Feed with a spoon or syringe

## Breakfast

Soft boiled eggs or fried eggs, or cream of wheat, or oatmeal, or soup. Serve with orange juice and milk. Coffee or tea.

## Lunch

Soup of any kind., 1 small container Activia or Greek yogurt, or Yoplait. Serve with probiotics drink or daweh or coffee or tea.

## Dinner

Harissa, Dolma mashed, mashed Kipteh mashed kubba hamouth, mashed chicken and rice or blend with some broth, any kabob and rice blended with some broth. Serve with herb tea like peach tea.

Supplement every meal with some smoothie.

## Snacks
-Any kind of Smoothie. You can make any Smoothie sweet with a touch of honey.
-Ice cream
-Frozen yogurt- any flavor especially strawberry, at room temperature. Feed with a spoon or syringe

Ice cream and cake-Blend melted ice cream and cake and feed with a spoon or syringe

Any yogurt or Activia-Feed with a spoon or blend 1 container of yogurt with 1/2 cup of milk

Apple pie-Blend 1 piece of apple pie and feed with a spoon and add vanilla ice cream.

Apple sauce-this is a good snack and I use apple sauce to crush mom's meds and blend them in the apple sauce.

# Ancient Assyrian Cuisine written on Clay Tablets

The three Assyrian clay tablets held by Yale University give us a historical reference and insight from which we can trace the source of our cooking techniques and ingredients.

## Oldest bread recipe
Mesopotamia (Assyria) circa 2300 BC

14 oz flour
1 cup water
1/2 teaspoon salt.

Mix the salt and flour and gradually add water, kneading into a smooth and consistent dough. Divide the dough into round patties. Cover the dough and let it sit overnight. The next day place the mounds in the oven and bake at 350 degrees Fahrenheit for 30 minutes.

The three tablets, which are currently held by Yale University, contain detailed recipes for stews (there's a gazelle one, if you're interested), plus the ancient pie recipe. We're not entirely sure what kinds of birds the recipe requires, but with its emphasis on the gizzards as well as the rest of the bird, "it's a testament to nose-to-tail eating:"

"Carefully lay out the fowls on a platter; spread over them the chopped pieces of gizzard and pluck, as well as the small sêpêtu breads which have been baked in the oven; sprinkle the whole with sauce, cover with the prepared crust and send to the table."

## "Babylonian Lamb with Licorice and Juniper Berries"

"Leg of mutton, but no other meat is used. Prepare water; add fat; dodder [wild licorice] (Anise) as desired; salt to taste; cypress [juniper berries]; onion; samidu [semolina]; cumin; coriander; leek and garlic, mashed with kisimmu [sour cream or yogurt]. It is ready to serve."

Ingredients:
- Leg of mutton
- Water
- Fat
- Wild licorice
- Salt
- Juniper Berries
- Onion (sliced)

- ○ Semolina
- ○ Cumin
- ○ Coriander
- ○ Leek and garlic (mashed)
- ○ Sour Cream or Yogurt

Combine wild licorice, cumin, coriander, leek, garlic, and salt in a shallow bowl. Set aside. Remove any gristle from the sheep fat. Begin boiling a pot of water over an open flame. While the water is still heating up, add several globs of fat to the water and stir until mixed. Add the mixture of wild licorice, cumin, coriander, leek, garlic, and salt to the water and bring to a boil.

Add the mutton. When the meat is cooked all the way through, remove the pot from the heat. Mix sour cream or yogurt into the broth and serve.

## Zamzaganu

"Scatter cut-up pieces of meat in a kettle and cook. Clean some baru and add to the kettle. Before removing the kettle from the fire, strain the cooking liquid and stir in mashed leek and garlic and a corresponding amount of raw suhutinnu."

Ingredients:
- ○ Partridge Meat (Chopped)
- ○ Dates
- ○ Leeks (mashed)
- ○ Garlic (mashed)
- ○ Turnips (sliced)
- ○ Water
- ○ Sheep fat

Instructions:
Remove any gristle from the sheep fat. Begin boiling a pot of water over an open flame. While the water is still heating up, add several globs of fat to the water and stir until mixed. When the water begins to boil, add the partridge meat and the dates.
When the meat is cooked all the way through, strain the fatty water into a bowl and set aside. Place the cooked meat and dates on a plate.

**Zukanda**:

"Meat is used. Prepare water; add fat; dill; suhutinnu; coriander; leek and garlic, bound with blood; a corresponding amount of kisimmu [sour cream or yogurt] and more garlic."
Our Best Guess of Ingredients:
- ○ Lamb meat
- ○ Water
- ○ Fat
- ○ Dill
- ○ Turnips
- ○ Coriander
- ○ Leeks (mashed)
- ○ Garlic (mashed)
- ○ Lamb's blood
- ○ Sour Cream or yogurt

Instructions:
In a bowl, mix the mashed leeks and garlic with lamb's blood. Remove any gristle from the fat. Begin boiling a pot of water over an open flame. While the water is still heating up, add several globs of fat to the water and stir until mixed. When the water comes to a boil, add the lamb meat, carrots, coriander, and the mixture of leeks, garlic, and blood. Remove from heat when the meat is cooked all the way through. Serve with a dollop of sour cream and garnish with slices of garlic.

Ashurnasirpal II with his queen enjoying a cup of wine in the garden

Cooks at work in the royal kitchens.
Relief from Ashurbanipal's palace at Nineveh 7th century BC.

# GLOSSARY OF TERMS AND LOCATION

| | |
|---|---|
| Tossed Salad | 112 |
| Treeda, cold yogurt soup | 107 |
| Turmeric chicken | 159 |
| Vegetable Kabob | 70 |
| Vegetarian Dolma | 85 |
| Walnut/Date Bars | 119 |
| Walnut Raisin Cake | 130 |
| Wine | 178-182 |
| Yakhnee, stew | 19 |
| Zulabia, dessert | 136 |
| Znood Al Sit-Kahe, dessert | 137 |

Ana and Israel Yonan my paternal grandparents who fled the genocide from Urmia and met and married in Baghdad, Iraq.

Benjamin and Sanam Putros who fled the genocide in Urmia and met and married in Baghdad, Iraq.

The Yonan family in Assyria-1964-two years before we left our homeland and moved to Morton Grove, Illinois

A quilt I made for the Yonan family

The Yonan Family in Assyria

From Left-Rabee Youab I Yonan, his wife Jean Yonan, his sister Aglanteen, cousin Wilma, and aunt Joanne, Jean's sister. Sitting on the carpet from right-Mary, the eldest, Ann-Margret, Edward, and baby William-1960

## THE YONAN FAMILY-1996

In las Vegas to celebrate mom and dad's 50th wedding anniversary. My parents were lucky enough to have celebrated their 65th wedding anniversary before dad passed away in 2011.  Below picture 1996: From left to right-William, Mary, Eddie, Jean, Youab, and Ann-Margret "Maggie" Yonan.

Cover photo-Papa Youab Yonan sitting at the head of the table and nana holding baby Joseph. Me in the purple, to the left of me my niece Holly, William's daughter, my brother in-law Nashuan peaking his head in, my sister Mary, his wife, mom Jean holding Mary and Nashuan's baby Joseph, Jasmine in the red velvet dress, little Terah in the black top, my son Sam the Ham, Nina in her summer dress, my brother William with a huge grin, Nashuan's mother Clementine waving her hand, my brother big Eddie, his wife Janet. We had all come from different cities for a visit and dad grilled the kabobs and made his famous cake for us. Nana Jean marinated all the meats, made the rice, the gillaleh, and the vegetable kabob. Papa and nana's house in Turlock-2004-2005

## Acknowledgements

I want to thank Gaby and Elizabeth Gabriel for contributing their Dobo recipe to this book.

I also want to thank Shoushan Tower for contributing her mother's recipe to this book. I'm sure her mother is very proud that she immortalized this Kashka recipe.

I want to thank my precious son, Shmoel, (Sam) for his contributions to this book as well as helping me take care of my mother, by putting his life on hold for mom and me. You are the best son a mother can have, and my best friend. Love you more than life itself.

I want to thank our housekeeper and my friend Trini who has taken half of the burden of caring for my mom and always being there to help me for a year now.

I have the utmost respect, love and appreciation for my mother, her life, her journey as a woman, wife, mother, and her outstanding cooking and baking talents. She has enriched my life in every way possible and I couldn't have been a good cook or a good mother, if it wasn't for her recipes and cooking style. God bless you with a long and healthy life mom. Love you eternally.

To my dearest dad, I thank you for choosing a woman like Jean Yonan to be my mother. You were an exemplary human being and my humanity as well as my son's is attributed to you and the standards you set as a human being. Thank you also for teaching me how to make a last minute, delicious cake. Love you eternally and miss you every single day of my life.

To my grandmothers, Anna and Sanam, thank you for the delicious food you passed on to our family. Love you eternally and may God bless your souls.

Made in the USA
Las Vegas, NV
17 January 2022